MACBETH

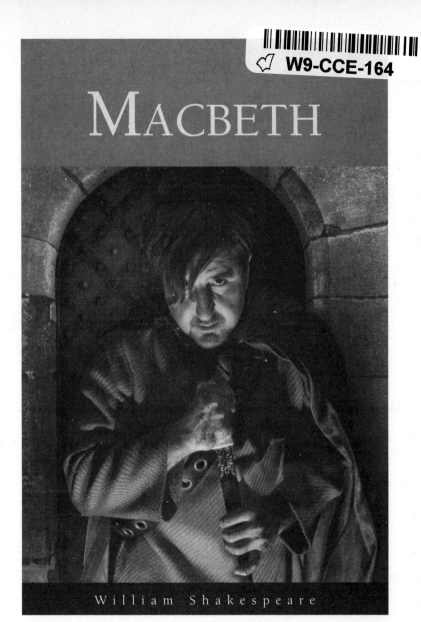

William Shakespeare

Prestwick House

LITERARY TOUCHSTONE CLASSICS

P.O. Box 658 Clayton, Delaware 19938 • www.prestwickhouse.com

SENIOR EDITOR: Paul Moliken

EDITOR: Daniel Reed

DESIGN: Jen Mendoza

PRODUCTION: Jerry Clark

Prestwick House
LITERARY TOUCHSTONE CLASSICS™
P.O. BOX 658 • CLAYTON, DELAWARE 19938
TEL: 1.800.932.4593
FAX: 1.888.718.9333
www.prestwickhouse.com

ISBN   978-1-58049-589-9

CONTENTS

Strategies for Understanding Shakespeare's Language

1. **When reading verse, note the appropriate phrasing and intonation.**

   DO NOT PAUSE AT THE END OF A LINE unless there is a mark of punctuation. Shakespearean verse has a rhythm of its own, and once a reader gets used to it, the rhythm becomes very natural to speak in and read. Beginning readers often find it helpful to read a short pause at a comma and a long pause for a period, colon, semicolon, dash, or question mark.

   Here's an example from *The Merchant of Venice*, Act IV, Scene i:

   > The quality of mercy is not strain'd, *(short pause)*
   > It droppeth as the gentle rain from heaven
   > Upon the place beneath: *(long pause)* it is twice blest; *(long pause)*
   > It blesseth him that gives, *(short pause)* and him that takes; *(long pause)*
   > 'Tis mightiest in the mighties; *(long pause)* it becomes
   > The throned monarch better than his crown; *(long pause)*

2. **Read from punctuation mark to punctuation mark for meaning.**

   In addition to helping you read aloud, punctuation marks define units of thought. Try to understand each unit as you read, keeping in mind that periods, colons, semicolons, and question marks signal the end of a thought. Here's an example from *The Taming of the Shrew*: Act I, Scene i:

   > Luc. Tranio, I saw her coral lips to move,
   >   And with her breath she did perfume the air;
   >   Sacred, and sweet, was all I saw in her.
   > Tra. Nay, then, 'tis time to stir him from his
   >   trance.
   >   I pray, awake, sir: if you love the maid,
   >   Bend thoughts and wits to achieve her.

   The first unit of thought is from "Tranio" to "air":
   He saw her lips move, and her breath perfumed the air.

   The second thought ("Sacred, and sweet...") re-emphasizes the first.

   Tranio replies that Lucentio needs to awaken from his trance and try to win "the maid." These two sentences can be considered one unit of thought.

3. In an **inverted sentence**, the verb comes before the subject. Some lines will be easier to understand if you put the subject first and reword the sentence. For example, look at the line below:

    "Never was seen so black a day as this:" (*Romeo and Juliet*, Act IV, Scene v)

    You can change its inverted pattern so it is more easily understood:

    "A day as black as this was never seen:"

4. An **ellipsis** occurs when a word or phrase is left out. In *Romeo and Juliet*, Benvolio asks Romeo's father and mother if they know the problem that is bothering their son. Romeo's father answers:

    *"I neither know it nor can learn of **him**"* (*Romeo and Juliet*, Act I, Scene i).

    This sentence can easily be understood to mean,

    "I neither know [the cause of] it,
    nor can [I] learn [about it from] him."

5. As you read longer speeches, keep track of the subject, verb, and object—*who* did *what* to *whom.*

    In the clauses below, note the subject, verbs, and objects:

    Ross: The king hath happily received, Macbeth,
          The news of thy success: and when he reads
          Thy personal venture in the rebel's fight… (*Macbeth*, Act I, Scene iii)

    1st clause: *The king hath happily received, Macbeth,/The news of thy success:*
    SUBJECT – The king
    VERB – has received
    OBJECT – the news [of Macbeth's success]
    2nd clause: *and when he reads/thy personal venture in the rebel's fight,*
    SUBJECT – he [the king]
    VERB – reads
    OBJECT – [about] your venture

    In addition to following the subject, verb, and object of a clause, you also need to track pronoun references. In the following soliloquy, Romeo, who is madly in love with Juliet, secretly observes her as she steps out on her balcony. To help you keep track of the pronoun references, we've made margin notes. (Note that the feminine pronoun sometimes refers to Juliet, but sometimes does not.)

But, soft! what light through yonder window breaks?
It is the east, and Juliet is the sun!
Arise, fair sun, and kill the envious moon,
Who* is already sick and pale with grief,   *"Who" refers to the moon.
That thou her* maid* art more fair than she:* *"thou her maid" refers
                                                to Juliet, the sun.
                                              *"she" and "her" refer to the moon.

In tracking the line of action in a passage, it is useful to identify the main thoughts that are being expressed and paraphrase them. Note the following passage in which Hamlet expresses his feelings about the death of his father and the remarriage of his mother:

O God! a beast that wants discourse of reason
Would have mourn'd longer—married with my uncle,
My father's brother, but no more like my father
Than I to Hercules. (*Hamlet*, Act I, Scene ii)

Paraphrasing the three main points, we find that Hamlet is saying:

- a mindless beast would have mourned the death of its mate longer than my mother did
- she married my uncle, my father's brother
- my uncle is not at all like my father

If you are having trouble understanding Shakespeare, the first rule is to read it out loud, just as an actor rehearsing would have to do. That will help you understand how one thought is connected to another.

6. Shakespeare frequently uses **metaphor** to illustrate an idea in a unique way. Pay careful attention to the two dissimilar objects or ideas being compared. In *Macbeth*, Duncan, the king says:

I have begun to plant thee, and will labour
To make thee full of growing. (*Macbeth*, Act I, Scene v)

The king compares Macbeth to a tree he can plant and watch grow.

7. An **allusion** is a reference to some event, person, place, or artistic work, not directly explained or discussed by the writer; it relies on the reader's familiarity with the item referred to. Allusion is a quick way of conveying information or presenting an image. In the following lines, Romeo alludes to Diana, goddess of the hunt and of chastity, and to Cupid's arrow (love).

ROMEO: Well, in that hit you miss: she'll not be hit
        with Cupid's arrow, she hath Dian's wit;
        and in strong proof of chastity well arm'd
        (*Romeo and Juliet*, Act I, Scene i)

8. Contracted words are words in which a letter has been left out. Some that frequently appear:

be't	on't	wi'
do't	t'	'sblood
'gainst	ta'en	i'
'tis	e'en	
'bout	know'st	'twill
	ne'er	o' o'er

9. Archaic, obsolete, and familiar words with unfamiliar definitions may also cause problems.

- **Archaic Words:** Some archaic words, like *thee, thou, thy,* and *thine,* are instantly understandable, while others, like *betwixt,* cause a momentary pause.

- **Obsolete Words:** If it were not for the notes in a Shakespeare text, obsolete words could be a problem; words like *beteem* are usually not found in student dictionaries. In these situations, however, a quick glance at the book's notes will solve the problem.

- **Familiar Words with Unfamiliar Definitions:** Another problem is those familiar words whose definitions have changed. Because readers think they know the word, they do not check the notes. For example, in this comment from *Much Ado About Nothing,* Act I, Scene i, the word *an* means "if":

BEATRICE: Scratching could not make it worse, *an* 'twere such
            a face as yours were.

For this kind of word, we have included margin notes.

10. Wordplay—puns, double entendres, and malapropisms:

- A **pun** is a literary device that achieves humor or emphasis by playing on ambiguities. Two distinct meanings are suggested either by the same word or by two similar-sounding words.

- A **double entendre** is a kind of pun in which a word or phrase has a second, usually sexual, meaning.

- A **malapropism** occurs when a character mistakenly uses a word that he or she has confused with another word. In *Romeo and Juliet,* the Nurse tells Romeo that she needs to have a "confidence" with him, when she should have said "conference." Mockingly, Benvolio then says she probably will "indite" (rather than "invite") Romeo to dinner.

7

11. **Shakespeare's Language:**

Our final word on Shakespeare's language is adapted by special permission from Ralph Alan Cohen's book *Shakesfear and How to Cure It—A Guide to Teaching Shakespeare.*

What's so hard about Shakespeare's language? Many students come to Shakespeare's language assuming that the language of his period is substantially different from ours. In fact, 98% of the words in Shakespeare are current-usage English words. So why does it sometimes seem hard to read Shakespeare? There are three main reasons:

- Originally, Shakespeare wrote the words for an actor to illustrate them as he spoke. In short, the play you have at hand was meant for the stage, not for the page.

- Shakespeare had the same love of reforming and rearranging words in such places as hip-hop and sportscasting today. His plays reflect an excitement about language and an inventiveness that becomes enjoyable once the reader gets into the spirit of it.

- Since Shakespeare puts all types of people on stage, those characters will include some who are pompous, some who are devious, some who are boring, and some who are crazy, and all of these will speak in ways that are sometimes trying. Modern playwrights creating similar characters have them speak in similarly challenging ways.

12. **Stage Directions:**

Shakespeare's stagecraft went hand-in-hand with his wordcraft. For that reason, we believe it is important for the reader to know which stage directions are modern and which derive from Shakespeare's earliest text—the single-play Quartos or the Folio, the first collected works (1623). All stage directions appear in italics, but the brackets enclose modern additions to the stage directions. Readers may assume that the unbracketed stage directions appear in the Quarto and/or Folio versions of the play.

13. **Scene Locations:**

Shakespeare imagined his plays, first and foremost, on the stage of his outdoor or indoor theatre. The original printed versions of the plays do not give imaginary scene locations, except when they are occasionally mentioned in the dialogue. As an aid to the reader, this edition *does* include scene locations at the beginning of each scene, but puts all such locations in brackets to remind the reader that *this is not what Shakespeare envisioned and only possibly what he imagined.*

Reading Pointers for Sharper Insights

1. Look for incidents or comments that support these major aspects of the play:

    - **Fate and Free Will**

      Throughout the play, Macbeth believes the prophecies of the witches, and he is willing to murder those who would interfere in the fulfillment of the predictions. Does Macbeth have choices in his destiny, or is he a pawn of the witches? Can he truly change anything in his future, or is he restricted to a specific destiny, despite any action he takes?

    - **The Various Types of Rulers**

      Characters in positions of influence and responsibility demonstrate several styles of leadership throughout the play. Try to determine what type of authority Duncan, Macbeth and Lady Macbeth, and Malcolm represent: tyrannical, regal, generous, democratic, etc. Does Macbeth fit the definition of a tragic hero?

    - **Ambition as Evil**

      Macbeth, at first a loyal and valiant servant to his king and country, finds himself caught in an unbreakable chain of events once he learns of his potential ascent to the throne. Why does Macbeth, a loyal and brave kinsman of Duncan's at the beginning of the play, become the embodiment of evil?

    - **Guilt and Fear**

      Is Macbeth troubled more by guilt over his evil acts or by fear of punishment? How do fear and guilt affect both him and Lady Macbeth?

2. Decide if Macbeth is inherently an evil person by considering what influences him more: his ambition, the prophecies of three witches, or Lady Macbeth's prodding. Why does he act as he does?

3. As you read, be aware of the following elements and terms, and note when each appears:

    allusion   metaphor   comic relief   personification

4. **Symbols**: As you read, consider how the following items relate to, emphasize, or change major themes in the play. What, or who, might each one represent?

blood	owls	martins	birds of prey
sleep	night	snakes	weather

5. **Styles of speech determined by characters' social status or emotional state**: Watch for changes in rhyme and meter, as well as changes from poetry to prose, and note which character is speaking when a change occurs.

MACBETH

William Shakespeare

DRAMATIS PERSONAE

DUNCAN, King of Scotland
MALCOLM, elder son of Duncan
DONALBAIN, younger son of Duncan

MACBETH, Thane of Glamis and Cawdor, a general in the King's army
LADY MACBETH, his wife

BANQUO, Thane of Lochaber, a general in the King's army
FLEANCE, his son
MACDUFF, Thane† of Fife, a nobleman of Scotland
LADY MACDUFF, his wife

LENNOX, nobleman of Scotland
ROSS, nobleman of Scotland
MENTEITH, nobleman of Scotland
ANGUS, nobleman of Scotland
CAITHNESS, nobleman of Scotland

SIWARD, Earl of Northumberland,† general of the English forces
YOUNG SIWARD, his son
SEYTON, attendant to Macbeth
Another Lord
An English Doctor
A Scottish Doctor
A Sergeant
Boy, Son of Macduff
Gentlewoman attending on Lady Macbeth
A Captain serving Duncan
A Porter
An Old Man
Three Murderers of Banquo
First Murderer at Macduff's castle
Messenger to Lady Macbeth
Messenger to Lady Macduff
Servant to Lady Macbeth
Servant to Lady Macduff
Three Witches or weird sisters
HECATE, Queen of the Witches
Three Apparitions†
(Lords, Gentlemen, Officers, Soldiers, Murderers, Attendants, and Messengers)

SCENE: Scotland and England

†Terms marked in the text with (†) can be looked up in the Glossary for additional information.

(handwritten: answers to the devil)

ACT I *(handwritten: MOOD: dark)*

SCENE I

[A desert place.]

Thunder and lightning. Enter three Witches.

FIRST WITCH: When shall we three meet again?
In thunder, lightning, or in rain? *(handwritten: tumultuous weather)*
SECOND WITCH: When the hurlyburly's[1] done; ¹turmoil
When the battle's lost and won. *(handwritten: rhyme)*
5 THIRD WITCH: That will be ere[2] the set of sun. ²before
FIRST WITCH: Where the place?
SECOND WITCH: Upon the heath.[3] ³a tract of open
land with sparse
vegetation
THIRD WITCH: There to meet with Macbeth.
FIRST WITCH: I come, Graymalkin.[4] ⁴the first witch's
familiar, an evil-
spirit servant in
the form of a cat
10 SECOND WITCH: Paddock[5] calls. Anon![6]
ALL: Fair is foul, and foul is fair.
Hover through the fog and filthy air. *Exeunt.* ⁵the second witch's
familiar, a toad

⁶Soon

(handwritten: sets the theme of the play dark, foreboding.)

SCENE II

[A camp near Forres.]

(handwritten: Norway / Scotland at war)

Alarum within. Enter King [Duncan], Malcolm, Donalbain,
Lennox, with Attendants, meeting a bleeding [Sergeant].

(handwritten: King duncan - King of scotland)

DUNCAN: What bloody man is that? He can report,
As seemeth by his plight, of the revolt *(handwritten: a victory for scot.)*
The newest state. *(handwritten: news of scotland/the war)*
MALCOLM: This is the sergeant,
5 Who, like a good and hardy soldier fought
'Gainst my captivity. Hail, brave friend!
Say to the King the knowledge of the broil[7] ⁷battle
As thou didst leave it. *(handwritten: state of the war)*

13

[8] exhausted

[9] i.e., drown each other

[10] Hebrides (islands west of Scotland and Ireland)†

[11] foot soldiers†

[12] armed horsemen†

[13] condemned

[14] i.e., granted him special favors

[15] Macdonwald

[16] cut him open

[17] navel

[18] jaw

[19] i.e., as after the equinox, there are storms

[20] fleeing

[21] king of Norway

[22] seeing an opportunity

[23] shining

[24] charges of gunpowder

[25] unless

[26] make the place memorable as

[27] the site where Jesus was crucified†

SERGEANT: Doubtful it stood,

10   As two spent[8] swimmers that do cling together
And choke their art.[9] The merciless Macdonwald—
Worthy to be a rebel, for to that
The multiplying villainies† of nature
Do swarm upon him—from the western isles[10]
15   Of kerns[11] and gallowglasses[12] is supplied;
And fortune, on his damned[13] quarrel smiling,
Show'd like a rebel's whore,[14] but all's too weak;
For brave Macbeth—well he deserves that name—
Disdaining fortune, with his brandish'd steel,
20   Which smoked with bloody execution,
Like valor's minion carved out his passage
Till he faced the slave,[15]
Which ne'er shook hands, nor bade farewell to him,
Till he unseam'd him[16] from the nave[17] to the chaps,[18]
25   And fix'd his head upon our battlements.

DUNCAN: O valiant cousin! Worthy gentleman!

SERGEANT: As whence the sun 'gins his reflection
Shipwrecking storms and direful thunders break,[19]
So from that spring whence comfort seem'd to come
30   Discomfort swells. Mark, King of Scotland, mark:
No sooner justice had, with valor arm'd,
Compell'd these skipping[20] kerns to trust their heels,
But the Norweyan lord,[21] surveying vantage,[22]
With furbish'd[23] arms and new supplies of men,
35   Began a fresh assault.

DUNCAN: Dismay'd not this
Our captains, Macbeth and Banquo?

SERGEANT: Yes,
As sparrows eagles, or the hare the lion.
40   If I say sooth, I must report they were
As cannons overcharged with double cracks,[24]
So they
Doubly redoubled strokes upon the foe.
Except[25] they meant to bathe in reeking wounds,
45   Or memorize[26] another Golgotha,[27]
I cannot tell—
But I am faint; my gashes cry for help.

[Handwritten annotations: "describing battle" · "Scottish winning but Macbeth got in the way" · "Macbeth respon" · "Killed many" · "Norwegian King attacks again" · "hes injured + need attention"]

DUNCAN: So well thy words become thee as thy wounds;
 They smack of honor both. Go get him surgeons.

[Exit attendant.]

50   Who comes here?

Enter Ross and Angus.

MALCOLM: The worthy Thane of Ross.
LENNOX: What a haste looks through his eyes! So should he look
 That seems to speak things strange.
55 ROSS: God save the King!
 DUNCAN: Whence camest thou, worthy Thane? *where did you come from*
 ROSS: From Fife, great King,
 Where the Norweyan banners flout[28] the sky
 And fan our people cold.[29]
60   Norway[30] himself, with terrible numbers,
 Assisted by that most disloyal traitor *traitor*
 The Thane of Cawdor, began a dismal conflict,
 Till that Bellona's bridegroom,[31] lapp'd in proof,[32]
 Confronted him with self-comparisons,[33]
65   Point[34] against point rebellious, arm 'gainst arm,
 Curbing his lavish[35] spirit; and, to conclude,
 The victory fell on us. *they won the battle*
 DUNCAN: Great happiness!
 ROSS: That now
70   Sweno, the Norways' king, craves composition;[36]
 Nor would we deign him burial of his men
 Till he disbursed, at Saint Colme's Inch,[37]
 Ten thousand dollars to our general use.
 DUNCAN: No more that Thane of Cawdor shall deceive
75   Our bosom interest.[38] Go pronounce his present[39] death,
 And with his former title greet Macbeth.
 ROSS: I'll see it done.
 DUNCAN: What he hath lost, noble Macbeth hath won.

Exeunt.

[28]*mock*

[29]*cold with fear*

[30]*the king of Norway*

[31]*Macbeth, described as the husband of the Roman goddess of war*

[32]*wearing impenetrable armor†*

[33]*equal deeds*

[34]*swordpoint*

[35]*wild*

[36]*a truce*

[37]*Inchcolm, an island†*

[38]*dearest concerns*

[39]*immediate*

Kill thane of Cawdor as traitor + give title to Macbeth

SCENE III
[A heath.]

Thunder. Enter the three Witches.

[handwritten: Casting spell on sailor]

FIRST WITCH: Where hast thou been, sister?

SECOND WITCH: Killing swine.

THIRD WITCH: Sister, where thou?

FIRST WITCH: A sailor's wife had chestnuts in her lap,

5   And mounch'd, and mounch'd, and mounch'd.
     "Give me," quoth I.
     "Aroint[40] thee, witch!" the rump-fed[41] ronyon[42] cries.
     Her husband's to Aleppo[43] gone, master o' the Tiger;[44]
     But in a sieve[45] I'll thither sail,

10   And, like a rat without a tail,
     I'll do, I'll do, and I'll do. *[handwritten: spells]*

SECOND WITCH: I'll give thee a wind.

FIRST WITCH: Thou'rt kind.

THIRD WITCH: And I another.

15   FIRST WITCH: I myself have all the other,[46]
     And the very ports they blow,
     All the quarters[47] that they know
     I' the shipman's card.[48]
     I will drain him dry as hay;

20   Sleep shall neither night nor day
     Hang upon his penthouse lid;[49]
     He shall live a man forbid.[50]
     Weary se'nnights[51] nine times nine
     Shall he dwindle, peak,[52] and pine;

25   Though his bark[53] cannot be lost,
     Yet it shall be tempest-tost.
     Look what I have.

SECOND WITCH: Show me, show me.

FIRST WITCH: Here I have a pilot's[54] thumb,

30   Wreck'd as homeward he did come.

Drum within.

THIRD WITCH: A drum, a drum!
     Macbeth doth come.

ALL: The weird[55] sisters, hand in hand,

[handwritten notes: spell; 7 weeks dry ports, rough waters but will not be lost]

Margin glosses:
40 Be gone
41 fed on rump meat
42 fat woman
43 A city in Syria and center of trade and Christianity in the Middle East during the middle ages
44 the husband's ship
45 basket
46 other winds
47 directions
48 compass card†
49 eyelid
50 cursed
51 weeks
52 waste away
53 ship
54 ship helmsman's
55 fate-manipulating
56 travelers

Posters[56] of the sea and land,

35   Thus do go about, about:

Thrice to thine, and thrice to mine,

And thrice again, to make up nine.

Peace! The charm's wound up.

Enter Macbeth and Banquo. *weather outside — won battle.*

MACBETH: So foul and fair a day I have not seen.

40   BANQUO: How far is't call'd[57] to Forres? What are these   [57]*said to be*

So wither'd, and so wild in their attire,

That look not like the inhabitants o' the earth,

And yet are on't? Live you? or are you aught[58] *are you*   [58]*anything*

That man may question?[59] You seem to understand me, *alive or ghosts*   [59]*speak with*

By each at once her choppy[60] finger laying   [60]*chapped, dry*

45   Upon her skinny lips. You should be women,

And yet your beards forbid me to interpret

That you are so.

MACBETH: Speak, if you can. What are you?

FIRST WITCH: All hail, Macbeth! hail to thee, Thane of

50   Glamis! *keeps title now*

SECOND WITCH: All hail, Macbeth! hail to thee, Thane of

Cawdor! *new title soon*

THIRD WITCH: All hail, Macbeth, that shalt be King hereafter! *will be king soon*

BANQUO: Good sir, why do you start, and seem to fear

55   Things that do sound so fair? I' the name of truth,

Are ye fantastical[61] or that indeed *are you real?*   [61]*imaginary*

Which outwardly ye show? My noble partner

You greet with present grace[62] and great prediction   [62]*title*

Of noble having[63] and of royal hope,   [63]*possessions*

60   That he seems rapt[64] withal. To me you speak not.   [64]*mesmerized*

If you can look into the seeds of time,

And say which grain will grow and which will not,

Speak then to me, who neither beg nor fear

Your favors nor your hate.

65   FIRST WITCH: Hail!

SECOND WITCH: Hail!

THIRD WITCH: Hail!

FIRST WITCH: Lesser than Macbeth, and greater.

SECOND WITCH: Not so happy,[65] yet much happier.   [65]*fortunate*

[66] beget

[67] unclear

[68] Macbeth's father's

70   THIRD WITCH: Thou shalt get[66] kings, though thou be none.
        So all hail, Macbeth and Banquo!
     FIRST WITCH: Banquo and Macbeth, all hail!
     MACBETH: Stay, you imperfect[67] speakers, tell me more.
        By Sinel's[68] death I know I am Thane of Glamis;
75   But how of Cawdor? The Thane of Cawdor lives,
        A prosperous gentleman; and to be King

(handwritten: disbelief / amazed)

        Stands not within the prospect of belief,
        No more than to be Cawdor. Say from whence

[69] information

        You owe this strange intelligence,[69] or why

[70] blighted; cursed

80   Upon this blasted[70] heath you stop our way
        With such prophetic greeting? Speak, I charge you.

(handwritten: where do you get this from)   [Witches vanish.]

     BANQUO: The earth hath bubbles as the water has,   _(handwritten: where are they going)_
        And these are of them. Whither are they vanish'd?

[71] physical

     MACBETH: Into the air, and what seem'd corporal[71] melted
85   As breath into the wind. Would they had stay'd!
     BANQUO: Were such things here as we do speak about?

[72] causing insanity

        Or have we eaten on the insane[72] root
        That takes the reason prisoner? _(handwritten: are we crazy)_
     MACBETH: Your children shall be kings.
90   BANQUO: You shall be King.
     MACBETH: And Thane of Cawdor too. Went it not so?
     BANQUO: To the selfsame tune and words. Who's here?

     [Enter Ross and Angus.]

[73] considers

     ROSS: The King hath happily received, Macbeth,
        The news of thy success; and when he reads[73]

[74] accomplishments

95   Thy personal venture[74] in the rebels' fight,
        His wonders and his praises do contend

[75] his amazement

        Which should be thine or his. Silenced with that,[75]
        In viewing o'er the rest o' the selfsame day,
        He finds thee in the stout Norweyan ranks,
100   Nothing afeard of what thyself didst make,

[76] methods

        Strange images[76] of death. As thick as hail

[77] messenger

        Came post[77] with post, and every one did bear
        Thy praises in his kingdom's great defense,
        And pour'd them down before him.
105 ANGUS: We are sent

To give thee, from our royal master, thanks;
Only to herald thee into his sight,
Not pay thee.
ROSS: And for an earnest[78] of a greater honor,
110   He bade me, from him, call thee Thane of Cawdor.
In which addition,[79] hail, most worthy Thane,
For it is thine.
BANQUO: What, can the devil speak true?
MACBETH: The Thane of Cawdor lives. Why do you dress me
115   In borrow'd robes?
ANGUS: Who was the Thane lives yet,
But under heavy judgement bears that life
Which he deserves to lose. Whether he was combined[80]
With those of Norway, or did line[81] the rebel
120   With hidden help and vantage,[82] or that with both
He labor'd in his country's wreck,[83] I know not;
But treasons capital, confess'd and proved,
Have overthrown him.
MACBETH: *[Aside.]* Glamis, and Thane of Cawdor! *2 things are true*
125   The greatest is behind.[84]   *[To Ross and Angus.]*
Thanks for your pains.   *[Aside to Banquo.]*
Do you not hope your children shall be kings,
When those that gave the Thane of Cawdor to me
Promised no less to them?
130 BANQUO: *[Aside to Macbeth.]* That, trusted home,[85] *you may be king*
Might yet enkindle you unto the crown,
Besides the Thane of Cawdor. But 'tis strange;
And oftentimes, to win us to our harm, *evil*
The instruments of darkness tell us truths,
135   Win us with honest trifles, to betray 's[86]
In deepest consequence—
Cousins, a word, I pray you.
MACBETH: *[Aside.]* Two truths are told,
As happy prologues[87] to the swelling act[88]
140   Of the imperial theme!—I thank you, gentlemen.
[Aside.] This supernatural soliciting[89]
Cannot be ill, cannot be good. If ill,
Why hath it given me earnest of success,
Commencing in a truth? I am Thane of Cawdor.
145   If good, why do I yield to that suggestion
Murder king duncan

[margin notes:]
[78]*pledge*
[79]*title*
[80]*allied*
[81]*assist*
[82]*advantage*
[83]*ruin*
[84]*yet to come*
[85]*entirely*
[86]*betray us*
[87]*predictions*
[88]*rising action*
[89]*temptation*

[90] *make my hair stand up*

[91] *custom*

[92] *in which*

[93] *self*

[94] *action*

[95] *speculation*

[96] *effort*

[97] *new*

[98] *fit*

[99] *wearer's body*

[100] *except*

[101] *wait*

[102] *pardon*

[103] *written to memory*

[104] *meantime*

Whose horrid image doth unfix my hair[90]
And make my seated heart knock at my ribs,
Against the use[91] of nature? Present fears
Are less than horrible imaginings:
150 My thought, whose[92] murder yet is but fantastical,
Shakes so my single state of man[93] that function[94]
Is smother'd in surmise,[95] and nothing is
But what is not.

BANQUO: Look, how our partner's rapt.

155 MACBETH: *[Aside.]* If chance will have me king, why, chance
may crown me
Without my stir.[96]

BANQUO: New honors come upon him,
Like our strange[97] garments, cleave[98] not to their mould[99]
160 But[100] with the aid of use.

MACBETH: *[Aside.]* Come what come may,
Time and the hour runs through the roughest day.

BANQUO: Worthy Macbeth, we stay[101] upon your leisure.

MACBETH: Give me your favor;[102] my dull brain was wrought
165 With things forgotten. Kind gentlemen, your pains
Are register'd[103] where every day I turn
The leaf to read them. Let us toward the king.
Think upon what hath chanced, and at more time,
The interim[104] having weigh'd it, let us speak
170 Our free hearts each to other.

BANQUO: Very gladly.

MACBETH: Till then, enough. Come, friends.

Exeunt.

SCENE IV

[Forres. The palace.]

Flourish. Enter King [Duncan], Lennox, Malcolm, Donalbain,
and Attendants.

[handwritten: did you kill cawdor yet]

DUNCAN: Is execution done on Cawdor? Are not
    Those in commission[105] yet return'd?

MALCOLM: My liege,
    They are not yet come back. But I have spoke

5   With one that saw him die, who did report *[handwritten: saw him killed + confessed]*
    That very frankly he confess'd his treasons,
    Implored your highness' pardon, and set forth *[handwritten: died w/ honor]*
    A deep repentance. Nothing in his life
    Became him like the leaving it; he died

10   As one that had been studied[106] in his death,
    To throw away the dearest thing he owed[107]
    As 'twere a careless[108] trifle.

DUNCAN: There's no art
    To find the mind's construction in the face:

15   He was a gentleman on whom I built *[handwritten:] Irony]*
    An absolute trust.

Enter Macbeth, Banquo, Ross, and Angus.
    O worthiest cousin!
    The sin of my ingratitude even now
    Was heavy on me. Thou art so far before,[109]

20   That swiftest wing of recompense is slow
    To overtake thee. Would thou hadst less deserved,
    That the proportion both of thanks and payment
    Might have been mine! Only I have left to say,
    More is thy due than more than all can pay.

25 MACBETH: The service and the loyalty I owe, *[handwritten: I did my job]*
    In doing it, pays itself. Your highness' part
    Is to receive our duties, and our duties
    Are to your throne and state, children and servants,
    Which do but what they should, by doing every thing

30   Safe[110] toward your love and honor.

DUNCAN: Welcome hither.
    I have begun to plant thee, and will labor

[handwritten: gave him the job + help him become more powerful]

[105]assigned to execute the Thane of Cawdor

[106]rehearsed

[107]owned

[108]worthless

[109]ahead

[110]in defense

To make thee full of growing. Noble Banquo,
That hast no less deserved, nor must be known
35 No less to have done so; let me enfold thee
And hold thee to my heart.
BANQUO: There if I grow,
   The harvest is your own. *loyalty*
DUNCAN: My plenteous joys,

[111]*luxurious*
40 Wanton[111] in fullness, seek to hide themselves
In drops of sorrow. Sons, kinsmen, thanes,

[112]*nearest in hierar- chy to the throne*
And you whose places are the nearest,[112] know
We will establish our estate[113] upon *Malcom will*

[113]*succession of heirs*
Our eldest, Malcolm, whom we name hereafter *be king*

[114]*the cottish heir to the throne*
45 The Prince of Cumberland;[114] which honor must *when h*
Macbeth Not unaccompanied invest[115] him only, *dies*

[115]*empower* *Must kill king +*
But signs of nobleness, like stars, shall shine
On all deservers. From hence to Inverness,[116]

[116]*Macbeth's castle*
Malcom And bind us further to you. *Macbeth's house*

[117]*i.e., rest becomes work if it is not done in your ser- vice*
50 MACBETH: The rest is labor which is not used for you:[117]
tell I'll be myself the harbinger,[118] and make joyful
my The hearing of my wife with your approach;

[118]*messenger who announces arrivals*
wife So humbly take my leave.
DUNCAN: My worthy Cawdor!

55 MACBETH: *[Aside.]* The Prince of Cumberland! That is a step
On which I must fall down, or else o'erleap,
For in my way it lies. Stars, hide your fires;
Let not light see my black and deep desires: *to be*

[119]*ignore*
The eye wink at[119] the hand; yet let that be *king*
60 Which the eye fears, when it is done, to see. *Exit.*
DUNCAN: True, worthy Banquo! He is full so valiant,
And in his commendations I am fed; *Macbeth*
It is a banquet to me. Let's after him,
Whose care is gone before to bid us welcome:
65 It is a peerless kinsman. *follow Macbeth*

Flourish. Exeunt.

SCENE V
Inverness. Macbeth's castle.

Enter Macbeth's wife alone, with a letter.

LADY MACBETH: "They met me in the day of success, and I have
learned by the perfectest report, they have more in them
than mortal knowledge. When I burned in desire to question them further, they made themselves air, into which
5   they vanished. Whiles I stood rapt in the wonder of it,
came missives[120] from the King, who all-hailed me 'Thane of
Cawdor'; by which title, before, these weird sisters saluted
me, and referred me to the coming on of time with 'Hail,
King that shalt be!' This have I thought good to deliver thee,
10   my dearest partner of greatness, that thou mightst not lose
the dues of rejoicing, by being ignorant of what greatness is
promised thee. Lay it to thy heart, and farewell."

   Glamis thou art, and Cawdor, and shalt be
   What thou art promised. Yet do I fear thy nature;
15   It is too full o' the milk of human kindness
   To catch the nearest way. Thou wouldst[121] be great;
   Art not without ambition, but without
   The illness[122] should attend it. What thou wouldst highly,
   That wouldst thou holily; wouldst not play false,
   And yet wouldst wrongly win. Thou'ldst have, great Glamis,
20   That which cries, "Thus thou must do, if thou have it;
   And that which rather thou dost fear to do
   Than wishest should be undone." Hie[123] thee hither,
   That I may pour my spirits in thine ear,
   And chastise with the valor of my tongue
25   All that impedes thee from the golden round,[124]
   Which fate and metaphysical[125] aid doth seem
   To have thee crown'd withal.[126]

Enter a Messenger.
   What is your tidings?
MESSENGER: The King comes here tonight.
30 LADY MACBETH: Thou'rt mad to say it!
   Is not thy master with him? who, were't so,

[120]*messengers*

[121]*would like to*

[122]*ruthlessness*

[123]*hurry*

[124]*crown*

[125]*supernatural*

[126]*with*

[handwritten marginal note: doesn't have the guts or horrible nastiness to do what he needs to do.]

[127]*i.e., outran*

[128]*a bird symbolic of impending evil*

[129]*remove my feminine qualities*

[130]*pangs of guilt†*
[131]*cruel*
[132]*bile†*
[133]*agents*
[134]*invisible*
[135]*assist*
[136]*cover*
[137]*darkest*

[138]*this moment*

[139]*deceive*
[140]*occasion*

Would have inform'd for preparation.

MESSENGER: So please you, it is true: our Thane is coming.
One of my fellows had the speed of[127] him,

35 Who, almost dead for breath, had scarcely more
Than would make up his message.

LADY MACBETH: Give him tending;
He brings great news.   *Exit Messenger.*
The raven[128] himself is hoarse

40 That croaks the fatal entrance of Duncan
Under my battlements. Come, you spirits
That tend on mortal thoughts, unsex me[129] here
And fill me, from the crown to the toe, top-full
Of direst cruelty! Make thick my blood,

45 Stop up the access and passage to remorse,
That no compunctious visitings of nature[130]
Shake my fell[131] purpose nor keep peace between
The effect and it! Come to my woman's breasts,
And take my milk for gall,[132] you murdering ministers,[133]

50 Wherever in your sightless[134] substances
You wait on[135] nature's mischief! Come, thick night,
And pall[136] thee in the dunnest[137] smoke of hell,
That my keen knife see not the wound it makes,
Nor heaven peep through the blanket of the dark

55 To cry, "Hold, hold!"

Enter Macbeth.
Great Glamis! Worthy Cawdor!
Greater than both, by the all-hail hereafter!
Thy letters have transported me beyond
This ignorant present, and I feel now

60 The future in the instant.[138]

MACBETH: My dearest love,
Duncan comes here tonight.

LADY MACBETH: And when goes hence?

MACBETH: Tomorrow, as he purposes.

65 LADY MACBETH: O, never
Shall sun that morrow see!
Your face, my Thane, is as a book where men
May read strange matters. To beguile[139] the time,[140]
Look like the time; bear welcome in your eye,

Plan to murder King!

70   Your hand, your tongue; look like the innocent flower,
      But be the serpent under't. He that's coming
      Must be provided for; and you shall put
      This night's great business into my dispatch,[141]   [141]*management*
      Which shall to all our nights and days to come
75   Give solely sovereign[142] sway and masterdom.   [142]*absolute*
  MACBETH: We will speak further.
  LADY MACBETH: Only look up clear;[143]   [143]*appear innocent*
      To alter favor[144] ever is to fear:[145]   [144]*the facial expression*
      Leave all the rest to me.   [145]*rouse suspicion*

                                           Exeunt.

SCENE VI
[Before Macbeth's castle.]
Hautboys[146] and torches.   [146]*loud wood-*
                                                                  wind instru-
                                                                  ments played to
                                                                  announce the
Enter King [Duncan], Malcolm, Donalbain, Banquo, Lennox,   *entrance of*
Macduff, Ross, Angus, and Attendants.   *royalty*

  DUNCAN: This castle hath a pleasant seat;[147] the air   [147]*location*
      Nimbly and sweetly recommends itself
      Unto our gentle senses.
  BANQUO: This guest of summer,   [148]*martin, a bird*
5   The temple-haunting martlet,[148] does approve[149]   *known to nest in*
      By his loved mansionry that the heaven's breath   *churches*
      Smells wooingly here. No jutty,[150] frieze,[151]   [149]*prove*
      Buttress,[152] nor coign of vantage,[153] but this bird   [150]*projection*†
      Hath made his pendant[154] bed and procreant cradle;[155]   [151]*a decorative band*
10   Where they most breed and haunt, I have observed   *along the top of a*
      The air is delicate.   *building*
                                                                  [152]*a stone or brick*
                                                                  support
Enter Lady Macbeth.
                                                                  [153]*a protruding*
                                                                  corner used as a
                                                                  lookout point
  DUNCAN: See, see, our honor'd hostess!   [154]*hanging*
      The love that follows us sometime is our trouble,[156]   [155]*place of breeding*
      Which still we thank[157] as love. Herein I teach you   [156]*inconvenience*
15   How you shall bid God 'ild[158] us for your pains,   [157]*appreciate*
      And thank us for your trouble.   [158]*yield (reward)*
  LADY MACBETH: All our service

[159]*Would be*

[160]*minor*

[161]*remain your beadsmen (monks who sold prayers for donations)*

[162]*followed him closely*

[163]*traveling attendant'*

[164]*helped*

[165]*trust from you*

[166]*accounts of what they own*

[167]*Ever ready*

[168]*what is yours*

[169]*With your permission*

In every point twice done, and then done double,
Were[159] poor and single[160] business to contend

20   Against those honors deep and broad wherewith
Your Majesty loads our house. For those of old,
And the late dignities heap'd up to them,
We rest your hermits.[161]

DUNCAN: Where's the Thane of Cawdor?

25   We coursed him at the heels[162] and had a purpose
To be his purveyor;[163] but he rides well,
And his great love, sharp as his spur, hath holp[164] him
To his home before us. Fair and noble hostess,
We are your guest tonight.

30   LADY MACBETH: Your servants ever
Have theirs, themselves, and what is theirs, in compt,[165]
To make their audit[166] at your Highness' pleasure,
Still[167] to return your own.[168]

DUNCAN: Give me your hand;

35   Conduct me to mine host. We love him highly,
And shall continue our graces towards him.
By your leave,[169] hostess.

Exeunt.

SCENE VII
Macbeth's castle.

Hautboys [and] torches. Enter a Sewer[170] and divers[171] Servants with dishes and service [who pass] over the stage. Then enter Macbeth.

[170]*Butler*

[171]*several*

[172]*catch (as with a net)*

[173]*its*

[174]*completion*

[175]*a sandbar surrounded by water*

[176]*punishment to endure*

[177]*because*

MACBETH: If it were done when 'tis done, then 'twere well
It were done quickly. If the assassination
Could trammel up[172] the consequence, and catch,
With his[173] surcease,[174] success; that but this blow

5   Might be the be-all and the end-all here,
But here, upon this bank and shoal[175] of time,
We'd jump the life to come. But in these cases
We still have judgment[176] here, that[177] we but teach
Bloody instructions, which being taught return

10   To plague the inventor. This even-handed[178] justice

      Commends the ingredients[179] of our poison'd chalice

      To our own lips. He's here in double trust:

      First, as I am his kinsman and his subject,

      Strong both against the deed; then, as his host,

15   Who should against his murderer shut the door,

      Not bear the knife myself. Besides, this Duncan

      Hath borne his faculties[180] so meek, hath been

      So clear[181] in his great office, that his virtues

      Will plead like angels trumpet-tongued against

20   The deep damnation of his taking-off,[182]

      And pity, like a naked new-born babe,

      Striding[183] the blast,[184] or heaven's cherubin[185] horsed

      Upon the sightless couriers of the air,[186]

      Shall blow the horrid deed in every eye,

25   That tears shall drown the wind. I have no spur

      To prick the sides of my intent, but only

      Vaulting ambition, which o'erleaps itself

      And falls on the other—

Enter Lady [Macbeth.]

      How now, what news?

30 LADY MACBETH: He has almost supp'd. Why have you left the

      chamber?

MACBETH: Hath he ask'd for me?

LADY MACBETH: Know you not he has?

MACBETH: We will proceed no further in this business:

35   He hath honor'd me of late, and I have bought[187]

      Golden opinions from all sorts of people,

      Which would be worn now in their newest gloss,

      Not cast aside so soon.

LADY MACBETH: Was the hope drunk

40   Wherein you dress'd yourself? Hath it slept since?

      And wakes it now, to look so green[188] and pale

      At what it did so freely? From this time

      Such I account thy love. Art thou afeard

      To be the same in thine own act and valor

45   As thou art in desire? Wouldst thou have that

      Which thou esteem'st the ornament of life

      And live a coward in thine own esteem,

[178]*impartial*

[179]*contents*

[180]*royal powers*

[181]*blameless; benevolent*

[182]*murder*

[183]*Riding*

[184]*storm*

[185]*(cherubim) angelic creatures*†

[186]*winds*

[187]*won*

[188]*sickly*

Letting "I dare not" wait upon "I would"
Like the poor cat i' the adage?[189]

50 MACBETH: Prithee, peace![190]
I dare do all that may become a man;
Who dares do more is none.[191]

LADY MACBETH: What beast was't then
That made you break[192] this enterprise to me?

55 When you durst[193] do it, then you were a man;
And, to be more than what you were, you would
Be so much more the man. Nor[194] time nor place
Did then adhere,[195] and yet you would make both:
They have made themselves, and that their fitness now

60 Does unmake you. I have given suck, and know
How tender 'tis to love the babe that milks me:
I would, while it was smiling in my face,
Have pluck'd my nipple from his boneless gums,
And dash'd the brains out, had I so sworn as you

65 Have done to this.

MACBETH: If we should fail?

LADY MACBETH: We fail?
But screw your courage to the sticking-place,[196]
And we'll not fail. When Duncan is asleep—

70 Whereto the rather[197] shall his day's hard journey
Soundly invite him—his two chamberlains[198]
Will I with wine and wassail[199] so convince,[200]
That memory, the warder[201] of the brain,
Shall be a fume, and the receipt[202] of reason

75 A limbec[203] only. When in swinish sleep
Their drenched[204] natures lie as in a death,
What cannot you and I perform upon
The unguarded Duncan? What not put upon
His spongy[205] officers, who shall bear the guilt

80 Of our great quell?[206]

MACBETH: Bring forth men-children only,
For thy undaunted mettle[207] should compose
Nothing but males. Will it not be received,
When we have mark'd with blood those sleepy two

85 Of his own chamber, and used their very daggers,
That they have done't?

LADY MACBETH: Who dares receive it other,

[189]*the cat that wanted fish but refused to get its feet wet*

[190]*silence*

[191]*not a man*

[192]*reveal*

[193]*dared*

[194]*Neither*

[195]*fit*

[196]*the notch on a crossbow that holds the taut string before firing*

[197]*Which will be as soon as*

[198]*bedroom attendants†*

[199]*drinking*

[200]*overpower*

[201]*keeper*

[202]*container*

[203]*part of a still into which the fumes rise*

[204]*drowsy*

[205]*drunken*

[206]*murder*

[207]*spirit*

As we shall make our griefs and clamor roar
Upon his death?

90 MACBETH: I am settled, and bend up
Each corporal agent[208] to this terrible feat.
Away, and mock the time with fairest show:
False face must hide what the false heart doth know.

Exeunt.

[208]*bodily strength*

M A C B E T H

ACT II

SCENE I

[Inverness. Court of Macbeth's castle.]

Enter Banquo, and Fleance, with a Torch* before him.

BANQUO: How goes the night, boy?

FLEANCE: The moon is down; I have not heard the clock.

BANQUO: And she goes down at twelve. *tired but*
can't sleep

FLEANCE: I take't 'tis later, sir.

5   BANQUO: Hold, take my sword. There's husbandry[1] in heaven.

Their candles are all out. Take thee that too. *Dark*

A heavy summons[2] lies like lead upon me, *night*

And yet I would not sleep. Merciful powers,[3] *unusual*

Restrain in me the cursed thoughts that nature *(something*

10   Gives way to in repose! *bad will happen)*

Enter Macbeth, and a Servant with a Torch.]

Give me my sword.

Who's there?

MACBETH: A friend.

BANQUO: What, sir, not yet at rest? The King's a-bed.

15   He hath been in unusual pleasure and *Duncan*

Sent forth great largess[4] to your offices:[5] *has been*

This diamond he greets your wife withal, *very generous*

By the name of most kind hostess, and shut up[6] *to*

In measureless content. *Macbeth*

20   MACBETH: Being unprepared, *+*

Our will became the servant to defect,[7] *to his*

Which else should free have wrought.[8] *wife*

BANQUO: All's well.

I dreamt last night of the three weird sisters: *Irony*

25   To you they have show'd some truth. *witches*

*"Torch" may indicate an attendant bearing a torch, rather than the torch itself.

[1]*careful saving*

[2]*sleepiness*

[3]*Guardian angels*

[4]*gifts; generosities*

[5]*servants*

[6]*went to sleep*

[7]*i.e., Our desire to please the king was overruled by our lack of supplies*

[8]*i.e., which otherwise we would freely have provided*

31

[handwritten: he is planning]

MACBETH: I think not of them: *[handwritten: Lies]*

    Yet, when we can entreat an hour to serve,[9]

    We would spend it in some words upon that business,

    If you would grant the time. *[handwritten: talk later]*

30 BANQUO: At your kind'st leisure.

MACBETH: If you shall cleave[10] to my consent,[11] when 'tis,

    It shall make honor for you.

BANQUO: So[12] I lose none

    In seeking to augment it, but still keep

35   My bosom franchised[13] and allegiance clear,[14]

    I shall be counsell'd.[15]

MACBETH: Good repose the while.

BANQUO: Thanks, sir, the like to you.

               Exeunt Banquo [and Fleance].

MACBETH: Go bid thy mistress, when my drink is ready,

40   She strike upon the bell. Get thee to bed.   *Exit [Servant].*

    Is this a dagger which I see before me, *[handwritten: hallucination]*

    The handle toward my hand? Come, let me clutch thee.

    I have thee not, and yet I see thee still.

    Art thou not, fatal vision, sensible[16]

45   To feeling as to sight? Or art thou but

    A dagger of the mind, a false creation,

    Proceeding from the heat-oppressed[17] brain?

    I see thee yet, in form as palpable *[handwritten: touchable]*

    As this which now I draw.

50   Thou marshall'st[18] me the way that I was going, *[handwritten: wants]*

    And such an instrument I was to use. *[handwritten: to kill duncan]*

    Mine eyes are made the fools o' the other senses,

[handwritten: bloody dagger = the deed is done]

    Or else worth all the rest. I see thee still,

    And on thy blade and dudgeon[19] gouts[20] of blood,

55   Which was not so before. There's no such thing:

    It is the bloody business which informs[21]

    Thus to mine eyes. Now o'er the one half-world

    Nature seems dead, and wicked dreams abuse[22]

    The curtain'd sleep; witchcraft celebrates

60   Pale Hecate's[23] offerings; and wither'd Murder,

    Alarum'd[24] by his sentinel, the wolf,

    Whose howl's his watch,[25] thus with his stealthy pace,

    With Tarquin's[26] ravishing strides, towards his design[27]

    Moves like a ghost. Thou sure and firm-set earth,

Marginal glosses:

[9] find a good time

[10] adhere

[11] advice

[12] As long as

[13] free of guilt

[14] pure

[15] open to your suggestion

[16] perceptible

[17] fevered

[18] guides

[19] handle

[20] drops

[21] makes shapes

[22] deceive

[23] the goddess of witchcraft[†]

[24] Alarmed

[25] cry

[26] the Roman prince who raped Lucrece[†]

[27] prey

hopefully no one will hear me

65 Hear not my steps, which way they walk, for fear
Thy very stones prate of my whereabout,
And take[28] the present horror[29] from the time,
Which now suits with it. Whiles I threat, he lives;
Words to the heat of deeds too cold breath gives.

[28]diminish

[29]*i.e.,* grim silence

A bell rings.

70 I go, and it is done: the bell invites me.
Hear it not, Duncan, for it is a knell
That summons thee to heaven, or to hell.

knell - death

Exit.

SCENE II
[The same.]

Enter Lady [Macbeth].

LADY MACBETH: That which hath made them drunk hath
made me bold; *now what they are drunk*
What hath quench'd them hath given me fire. Hark! Peace! *she feels bold, she drank too*
It was the owl that shriek'd, the fatal bellman,[30]

[30]*night watchman*

5 Which gives the stern'st good-night.[31] He is about it:
The doors are open, and the surfeited[32] grooms[33]
Do mock their charge[34] with snores: I have drugg'd their
     possets,[35]
That death and nature do contend about them,

[31]*i.e., death knell (a bell tolled on the evenings before executions)*

[32]*overindulged*

[33]*guards*

10 Whether they live or die.

[34]*duty*

Enter Macbeth

[35]*drinks of milk and liquor*

MACBETH: Who's there? what, ho!
LADY MACBETH: Alack, I am afraid they have awaked *Lady M would*
And 'tis not done. The attempt and not the deed *have done it if*
Confounds[36] us. Hark! I laid their daggers ready; *it hadn't looked*

[36]*ruins*

15 He could not miss 'em. Had he not resembled *like her father*
My father as he slept, I had done't. *Macbeth is*
My husband! *doing the murdering*
MACBETH: I have done the deed. Didst thou not hear a noise?
LADY MACBETH: I heard the owl scream and the crickets cry.
20 Did not you speak?

given himself over to evil.

If they couldn't pray they were cursed or bewitched Macbeth is flustered and afraid.

MACBETH: When?

LADY MACBETH: Now.

MACBETH: As I descended?

LADY MACBETH: Ay.

25 MACBETH: Hark!
     Who lies i' the second chamber?

LADY MACBETH: Donalbain.

MACBETH: This is a sorry sight.

LADY MACBETH: A foolish thought, to say a sorry sight.

30 MACBETH: There's one did laugh in's sleep, and one cried,
     "Murder!"
     That they did wake each other: I stood and heard them:
     But they did say their prayers and address'd them[37]
     Again to sleep.

35 LADY MACBETH: There are two lodged together.

MACBETH: One cried, "God bless us!" and "Amen" the other,
     As[38] they had seen me with these hangman's[39] hands.
     Listening their fear, I could not say "Amen,"
     When they did say "God bless us!"

40 LADY MACBETH: Consider it not so deeply.

MACBETH: But wherefore could not I pronounce "Amen"?
     I had most need of blessing, and "Amen"
     Stuck in my throat.

LADY MACBETH: These deeds must not be thought
     After these ways; so, it will make us mad.

45 MACBETH: Me thought I heard a voice cry "Sleep no more!
     Macbeth doth murder sleep"—the innocent sleep,
     Sleep that knits up the ravell'd[40] sleave of care,
     The death of each day's life, sore labor's bath,

50   Balm of hurt minds, great nature's second[41] course,
     Chief nourisher in life's feast—

LADY MACBETH: What do you mean?

MACBETH: Still it cried, "Sleep no more!" to all the house;
     "Glamis hath murdered sleep, and therefore Cawdor

55   Shall sleep no more. Macbeth shall sleep no more."

LADY MACBETH: Who was it that thus cried? Why, worthy
        Thane,
     You do unbend[42] your noble strength, to think
     So brainsickly of things. Go, get some water

60   And wash this filthy witness[43] from your hand.

Wont sleep again because of guilt

[37] themselves

[38] As though

[39] bloody [Hangmen had the task of disemboweling and quartering the bodies of the executed.]

[40] unravelled

[41] most nourishing [Customarily, the second course was the largest.]

[42] loosen

[43] evidence

Why did you bring these daggers from the place?
They must lie there. Go carry them, and smear
The sleepy grooms with blood.

MACBETH: I'll go no more:

65   I am afraid to think what I have done;
Look on't again I dare not.

LADY MACBETH: Infirm[44] of purpose![45]
Give me the daggers. The sleeping and the dead
Are but as pictures; 'tis the eye of childhood

70   That fears a painted devil. If he do bleed,
I'll gild[46] the faces of the grooms withal,[47]
For it must seem their guilt.

                         Exit. Knocking within.

[handwritten: dead are just like paintings]

MACBETH: Whence is that knocking?
How is't with me, when every noise appals[48] me?

75   What hands are here? Ha, they pluck out mine eyes!
Will all great Neptune's[49] ocean wash this blood
Clean from my hand? No, this my hand will rather
The multitudinous[50] seas incarnadine,[51]
Making the green one red.

[Re]-enter Lady [Macbeth.]

80 LADY MACBETH: My hands are of your color, but I shame
To wear a heart so white.   *Knock*

[handwritten: i would rather not be a coward]

I hear a knocking
At the south entry. Retire we to our chamber.

85   A little water clears us of this deed:
How easy is it then! Your constancy[52]
Hath left you unattended.[53]

[handwritten: your mind has left you]

                           Knock

Hark! more knocking:
Get on your nightgown, lest occasion[54] call us

90   And show us to be watchers.[55] Be not lost
So poorly in your thoughts.

MACBETH: To know my deed, 'twere best not know myself.

[handwritten: I feel guilty]*

                           Knock

Wake Duncan with thy knocking! I would thou couldst!

                           Exeunt.

[handwritten: his conscience is bothering him.]

---

[44] *weak*

[45] *will*

[46] *cover as with gold leaf*

[47] *with Duncan's blood*

[48] *makes me pale with fear*

[49] *the Roman god of the sea*

[50] *vast*

[51] *make red*

[52] *strength of will*

[53] *deserted*

[54] *the situation*

[55] *awake*

[handwritten margin notes: equivocation / unequivocal]

SCENE III
[The same.]

Enter a Porter.[56] *Knocking within.*

[handwritten note: angry, drunk, someone is bothering him, pretends he is the doorman to hell!]

PORTER: Here's a knocking indeed! If a man were porter of
hell-gate, he should have old[57] turning the key.

Knock

Knock, knock, knock! Who's there, i' the name of
Belzebub?[58] Here's a farmer that hanged himself on th'
5   expectation of plenty.[59] Come in time![60] Have napkins[61]
enow about you; here you'll sweat for't.

Knock

Knock, knock! Who's there, in th' other devil's name?
[handwritten note: liar] Faith, here's an equivocator[62] that could swear in both the
scales against either scale, who committed treason enough
10   for God's sake, yet could not equivocate to heaven. O,
come in, equivocator.

Knock

Knock, knock, knock! Who's there? Faith, here's an
English tailor come hither, for stealing out of a French
hose.[63] Come in, tailor; here you may roast your goose.[64]

Knock

15   Knock, knock! Never at quiet! What are you? But this
place is too cold for hell. I'll devil-porter it no further. I
had thought to have let in some of all professions, that go
the primrose[65] way to the everlasting bonfire.[66]

Knock

Anon,[67] anon! I pray you, remember the porter.

[Opens the gate.]

Enter Macduff and Lennox.

20   MACDUFF: Was it so late, friend, ere you went to bed,
      That you do lie so late?
    PORTER: Faith, sir, we were carousing till the second cock:[68]
      and drink, sir, is a great provoker of three things.
    MACDUFF: What three things does drink especially provoke?
25   PORTER: Marry,[69] sir, nose-painting,[70] sleep, and urine.

---

[56] gatekeeper

[57] plenty of

[58] a devil

[59] surplus, which would lower the price of his goods

[60] Just in time

[61] handkerchiefs

[62] one who intentionally speaks vaguely†

[63] tight breeches

[64] heat your iron

[65] flowery; pleasurable [A primrose is a wildflower.]

[66] hell

[67] in good time

[68] 3:00 am

[69] by the Virgin Mary (an oath)

[70] reddening of the nose

sex

Lechery, sir, it provokes and unprovokes: it provokes the desire, but it takes away the performance. Therefore much drink may be said to be an equivocator with lechery: it makes him,[71] and it mars[72] him; it sets him on and it takes

30   him off; it persuades him and disheartens him; makes him stand to and not stand to; in conclusion, equivocates him in a sleep, and giving him the lie,[73] leaves him.

MACDUFF: I believe drink gave thee the lie[74] last night.

PORTER: That it did, sir, i' the very throat on[75] me: but I requited

35   him for his lie, and, I think, being too strong for him, though he took up my legs sometime, yet I made a shift[76] to cast[77] him.

Enter Macbeth.

MACDUFF: Is thy master stirring?

Our knocking has awaked him; here he comes.

40 LENNOX: Good morrow, noble sir.

MACBETH: Good morrow, both.

MACDUFF: Is the King stirring, worthy Thane?   *equivocation*

MACBETH: Not yet.

MACDUFF: He did command me to call timely[78] on him;

45   I have almost slipp'd the hour.

MACBETH: I'll bring you to him.

MACDUFF: I know this is a joyful trouble to you;

But yet 'tis one.

MACBETH: The labor we delight in physics[79] pain.

50   This is the door.

MACDUFF: I'll make so bold to call,

For 'tis my limited[80] service.   *Exit, Macduff.*

LENNOX: Goes the King hence today?

MACBETH: He does: he did appoint[81] so.

55 LENNOX: The night has been unruly. Where we lay,

Our chimneys were blown down, and, as they say,

Lamentings heard i' the air, strange screams of death,

And prophesying with accents terrible

Of dire combustion[82] and confused events

60   New hatch'd to the woeful time. The obscure bird[83]

Clamor'd the livelong night. Some say the earth

Was feverous and did shake.

---

[71] helps

[72] hurts

[73] [He puns on lie, meaning "fall down," and lye, a word for urine.]

[74] accuse you of lying; also, made you lie down

[75] of

[76] move

[77] "throw off," but also "vomit"

[78] early

[79] relieves

[80] specified

[81] plan

[82] chaos

[83] owl, the bird of darkness

—bad storm

MACBETH: 'Twas a rough night.

LENNOX: My young remembrance cannot parallel
65   A fellow to it.

[Re]-enter Macduff.

MACDUFF: O horror, horror, horror! Tongue nor heart
      Cannot conceive nor name thee.

MACBETH: ⎫
LENNOX: ⎬ What's the matter?

[84]*destruction*

70 MACDUFF: Confusion[84] now hath made his masterpiece.
      Most sacrilegious Murder hath broke ope

[85]*Duncan's body*
[Kings were believed
to have been
anointed by God.]

      The Lord's anointed temple[85] and stole thence
      The life o' the building.

MACBETH: What is't you say? the life?

75 LENNOX: Mean you his Majesty?

[86]*a monster who*
turned anyone
who looked at her
into stone†

MACDUFF: Approach the chamber, and destroy your sight
      With a new Gorgon.[86] Do not bid me speak;
      See, and then speak yourselves.   (Awake, awake!)
                              Exeunt Macbeth and Lennox.

Things are
Never as they
seem

      Ring the alarum bell. Murder and treason!
80   Banquo and Donalbain! Malcolm, awake!
      Shake off this downy sleep, death's counterfeit,
      And look on death itself! Up, up, and see

[87]*doomsday*

      The great doom's[87] image! Malcolm! Banquo!
      As from your graves rise up, and walk like sprites,

[88]*verify*

85   To countenance[88] this horror! Ring the bell.
                                    Bell rings.

Enter Lady [Macbeth.]

[89]*a discussion or*
conference

LADY MACBETH: What's the business,
      That such a hideous trumpet calls to parley[89]
      The sleepers of the house? Speak, speak!

MACDUFF: O gentle lady,
      'Tis not for you to hear what I can speak:

[90]*report*

90   The repetition[90] in a woman's ear
      Would murder as it fell.

Enter Banquo.

      O Banquo, Banquo!
      Our royal master's murdered.

LADY MACBETH: Woe, alas!

95 What, in our house?

BANQUO: Too cruel anywhere.

Dear Duff, I prithee, contradict thyself,
And say it is not so.

[Re]-enter Macbeth, Lennox, Ross.

MACBETH: Had I but died an hour before this chance,[91]
100 I had lived a blessed time; for from this instant
There's nothing serious in mortality:[92]
All is but toys; renown and grace is dead;
The wine of life is drawn, and the mere lees[93]
Is left[94] this vault[95] to brag of.

Enter Malcolm and Donalbain.

105 DONALBAIN: What is amiss?

MACBETH: You are, and do not know't:
The spring, the head, the fountain of your blood
Is stopp'd; the very source of it is stopp'd.

MACDUFF: Your royal father's murdered.

110 MALCOLM: O, by whom?

LENNOX: Those of his chamber, as it seem'd, had done't:
Their hands and faces were all badged[96] with blood;
So were their daggers, which unwiped we found
Upon their pillows:
115 They stared, and were distracted; no man's life
Was to be trusted with them.

MACBETH: O, yet I do repent me of my fury,
That I did kill them.

MACDUFF: Wherefore did you so?

120 MACBETH: Who can be wise, amazed, temperate and furious,
Loyal and neutral, in a moment? No man:
The expedition[97] of my violent love
Outrun the pauser[98] reason. Here lay Duncan,
His silver skin laced with his golden blood,
125 And his gash'd stabs look'd like a breach in nature
For ruin's wasteful[99] entrance: there, the murderers,
Steep'd in the colors of their trade, their daggers
Unmannerly breech'd[100] with gore. Who could refrain,
That had a heart to love, and in that heart

[91] *event*
[92] *life*
[93] *dregs*
[94] *left to*
[95] *wine cellar*
[96] *marked*
[97] *haste*
[98] *hesitant*
[99] *destroying*
[100] *covered*

130   Courage to make's love known? *taunts to distract Macbeth*
        LADY MACBETH: Help me hence, ho!
        MACDUFF: Look to the lady.
        MALCOLM: [Aside to Donalbain.] Why do we hold our
            tongues,
135   That most may claim this argument for ours?
        DONALBAIN: [Aside to Malcolm.] What should be spoken
            here, where our fate,
        Hid in an auger-hole,[101] may rush and seize us?
        Let's away;
140   Our tears are not yet brew'd.
        MALCOLM: [Aside to Donalbain.] Nor our strong sorrow
        Upon the foot of motion.[102]
        BANQUO: Look to the lady:
        And when we have our naked frailties hid,[103]
145   That suffer in exposure, let us meet
        And question[104] this most bloody piece of work
        To know it further. Fears and scruples[105] shake us:
        In the great hand of God I stand, and thence
        Against the undivulged pretence[106] I fight
150   Of treasonous malice.
        MACDUFF: And so do I.
        ALL: So all.
        MACBETH: Let's briefly[107] put on manly readiness[108]
        And meet i' the hall together.
155   ALL: Well contented.
                    Exeunt [all but Malcolm and Donalbain].
        MALCOLM: What will you do? Let's not consort with them:
        To show an unfelt sorrow is an office[109]
        Which the false man does easy. I'll to England.
        DONALBAIN: To Ireland, I; our separated fortune
160   Shall keep us both the safer. Where we are
        There's daggers in men's smiles: the near in blood,[110]
        The nearer bloody. *they could be the killers looking to kill them*
        MALCOLM: This murderous shaft[111] that's shot
        Hath not yet lighted,[112] and our safest way
165   Is to avoid the aim. Therefore to horse;
        And let us not be dainty of[113] leave-taking,
        But shift[114] away. There's warrant[115] in that theft
        Which steals[116] itself when there's no mercy left.
                                                Exeunt.

[101] small nook

[102] i.e., Our sorrow must wait until we have escaped.

[103] clothed

[104] discuss

[105] doubts

[106] secret motives for the murder

[107] quickly

[108] appropriate clothing and mindset

[109] action

[110] royal lineage

[111] arrow (assassination plot)

[112] landed (been completed)

[113] polite about

[114] sneak

[115] justification

[116] flees

SCENE IV
[Outside Macbeth's castle.]

Enter Ross, with an Old Man.

OLD MAN: Threescore and ten[117] I can remember well:
　　Within the volume of which time I have seen
　　Hours dreadful and things strange, but this sore night
　　Hath trifled former knowings.[118]

[117]*seventy years*

[118]*previous experience*

5　ROSS: Ah, good father,
　　Thou seest the heavens, as troubled with man's act,
　　Threaten his bloody stage. By the clock 'tis day,
　　And yet dark night strangles the travelling lamp.[119]
　　Is't night's predominance,[120] or the day's shame,

day but dark

[119]*sun*

[120]*rise to power*

10　That darkness does the face of earth entomb,
　　When living light should kiss it?
　OLD MAN: 'Tis unnatural,
　Even like the deed that's done. On Tuesday last
　　A falcon towering in her pride of place[121]

a smaller bird attacked the larger bird

[121]*at the highest point of flight*

15　Was by a mousing[122] owl hawk'd at[123] and kill'd.
　ROSS: And Duncan's horses—a thing most strange and
　　　certain—
　　Beauteous and swift, the minions[124] of their race,
　　Turn'd wild in nature, broke their stalls, flung out,

[122]*mouse-eating*

[123]*attacked*

[124]*finest examples*

20　Contending 'gainst obedience, as they would make
　　War with mankind.
　OLD MAN: 'Tis said they eat each other.
　ROSS: They did so, to the amazement of mine eyes
　　That look'd upon't.

Duncans horses got out and ate each other

Enter Macduff.

25　Here comes the good Macduff.
　　How goes the world, sir, now?
　MACDUFF: Why, see you not?
　ROSS: Is't known who did this more than bloody deed?
　MACDUFF: Those that Macbeth hath slain.

30　ROSS: Alas, the day!
　　What good[125] could they pretend?[126]
　MACDUFF: They were suborn'd:[127]
　　Malcolm and Donalbain, the King's two sons,

[125]*gain*

[126]*hope to receive*

[127]*bribed*

Are stol'n away and fled, which puts upon them

35 Suspicion of the deed.

ROSS: 'Gainst nature still!

[128]profitless   Thriftless[128] ambition, that wilt ravin up[129]

[129]devour   Thine own life's means! Then 'tis most like

The sovereignty will fall upon Macbeth.

[130]the ancient city where Scottish kings were crowned

40 MACDUFF: He is already named, and gone to Scone[130]

To be invested.[131]

[131]crowned king

ROSS: Where is Duncan's body?

MACDUFF: Carried to Colmekill,[132]

[132]the island where Scottish kings were buried

The sacred storehouse of his predecessors

45 And guardian of their bones.

ROSS: Will you to Scone?

[133]Macduff's castle

MACDUFF: No, cousin, I'll to Fife.[133]

ROSS: Well, I will thither.

MACDUFF: Well, may you see things well done there, Adieu,

50 Lest our old robes sit easier than our new!

ROSS: Farewell, father.

[134]blessing

OLD MAN: God's benison[134] go with you and with those

That would make good of bad and friends of foes!

Exeunt.

[Handwritten margin notes: "Macbeth will be king", "sceptre", "fair is foul, foul is fair."]

ACT III

SCENE I

[Forres. The palace.]

Enter Banquo.

[handwritten: soliloquy?]

BANQUO: Thou hast it now: King, Cawdor, Glamis, all,
  As the weird women promised, and I fear
  Thou play'dst most foully for't: yet it was said
  It should not stand in thy posterity,[1]
5 But that myself should be the root and father
  Of many kings. If there come truth from them—
  As upon thee, Macbeth, their speeches shine—
  Why, by the verities on thee made good,
  May they not be my oracles as well
10 And set me up in hope? But hush, no more.

[handwritten: suspects Macbeth had a hand in Duncans death]

[1] *descendants*

Sennet[2] sounded. Enter Macbeth as King, Lady [Macbeth as Queen], Lennox, Ross, Lords, and Attendants.

[2] *trumpet flourish*

MACBETH: Here's our chief guest.
LADY MACBETH: If he had been forgotten,
  It had been as a gap in our great feast
  And all-thing[3] unbecoming.

[3] *completely*

15 MACBETH: Tonight we hold a solemn supper, sir,
  And I'll request your presence.

[handwritten: wants banquo to come]

BANQUO: Let your Highness
  Command upon me, to the which my duties
  Are with a most indissoluble tie
20 Forever knit.
MACBETH: Ride you this afternoon?
BANQUO: Ay, my good lord.
MACBETH: We should have else desired your good advice,

[4] *always*

[5] *serious*

[6] *faster*

[7] *two*

[8] *staying*

[9] *lies*

[10] *state affairs*

[11] *Requiring*

[12] *together*

[13] *Until*

[14] *a title used to address servants*

[15] *outside*

[16] *king*

[17] *nobility*

[18] *added to*

[19] *made to seem less*

[20] *[Mark Antony and Octavius Caesar were leaders of Rome; Caesar was considered greater than Antony.]†*

[21] *witches*

       Which still[4] hath been both grave[5] and prosperous
25   In this day's council; but we'll take tomorrow.
       Is't far you ride?
BANQUO: As far, my lord, as will fill up the time
       'Twixt this and supper. Go not my horse the better,[6]
       I must become a borrower of the night
30   For a dark hour or twain.[7]
MACBETH: Fail not our feast.
BANQUO: My lord, I will not.
MACBETH: We hear our bloody cousins are bestow'd[8]
       In England and in Ireland, not confessing
35   Their cruel parricide, filling their hearers
       With strange invention.[9] But of that tomorrow,
       When therewithal we shall have cause of state[10]
       Craving[11] us jointly.[12] Hie you to horse; adieu,
       Till you return at night. Goes Fleance with you?
40 BANQUO: Ay, my good lord. Our time does call upon's.
MACBETH: I wish your horses swift and sure of foot,
       And so I do commend you to their backs.
       Farewell.   *Exit Banquo.*
       Let every man be master of his time
45   Till seven at night; to make society
       The sweeter welcome, we will keep ourself
       Till supper time alone. While[13] then, God be with you!
              Exeunt Lords[and Lady Macbeth].
       Sirrah,[14] a word with you. Attend those men
       Our pleasure?
50 SERVANT: They are, my lord, without[15] the palace gate.
MACBETH: Bring them before us.   *Exit Servant.*
       To be thus[16] is nothing,
       But to be safely thus. Our fears in Banquo
       Stick deep, and in his royalty[17] of nature
55   Reigns that which would be fear'd. 'Tis much he dares,
       And, to[18] that dauntless temper of his mind,
       He hath a wisdom that doth guide his valor
       To act in safety. There is none but he
       Whose being I do fear; and under him
60   My genius is rebuked,[19] as it is said
       Mark Antony's was by Caesar.[20] He chid the sisters,[21]
       When first they put the name of King upon me,

[Handwritten annotations: "Meet tomorrow"; "Malcom + Donal killing their father"; "Banquo's son"; "party at 7:00"; "leave Macbeth alone"; "are the men here nervous"; "no good nature, wisdom + bravery"; "worried about Banquo"; "To be King is nothing, unless I am safely King."]

And bade them speak to him; then prophet-like
They hail'd him father to a line of kings:
65 Upon my head they placed a fruitless[22] crown   [22]*sterile*
And put a barren sceptre in my gripe,   [23]*not related*
Thence to be wrench'd with an unlineal[23] hand,   [24]*defiled*
No son of mine succeeding. If't be so,
For Banquo's issue have I filed[24] my mind,   [25]*bitterness; deep-*
70 For them the gracious Duncan have I murdered,   *seated resentment*
Put rancors[25] in the vessel of my peace   [26]*soul*
Only for them, and mine eternal jewel[26]   [27]*devil*
Given to the common enemy of man,[27]   [28]*combat arena*
To make them kings, the seed of Banquo kings!
75 Rather than so, come, Fate, into the list,[28]   [29]*do battle with*
And champion[29] me to the utterance![30] Who's there?   [30]*last word (death)*

[Re]-enter Servant and two Murderers.
Now go to the door, and stay there till we call.

Exit Servant.

Was it not yesterday we spoke together?
FIRST MURDERER: It was, so please your Highness.
80 MACBETH: Well then, now
Have you consider'd of my speeches? Know
That it was he, in the times past, which held you
So under fortune, which you thought had been
Our innocent self? This I made good to you
85 In our last conference, pass'd[31] in probation[32] with you   [31]*reviewed*
How you were borne in hand,[33] how cross'd,[34] the instruments,[35]   [32]*proof*
Who wrought with them, and all things else that might   [33]*deceived*
To half a soul and to a notion[36] crazed   [34]*shut out*
Say, "Thus did Banquo."   [35]*agents*
90 FIRST MURDERER: You made it known to us.   [36]*mind*
MACBETH: I did so, and went further, which is now
Our point of second meeting. Do you find
Your patience so predominant in your nature,
That you can let this go? Are you so gospell'd,[37]   [37]*[In the New*
95 To pray for this good man and for his issue,   *Testament, Jesus*
Whose heavy hand hath bow'd you to the grave   *advises that men*
And beggar'd yours[38] forever?   *love and forgive*
FIRST MURDERER: We are men, my liege.   *their enemies.]*
MACBETH: Ay, in the catalogue[39] ye go for men,   [38]*your family*
                                                             [39]*list*

[40] mastiffs (large watchdogs)

[41] shaggy dogs

[42] dogs used for hunting waterfowl

[43] wolf-dog cross-breeds

[44] called

[45] a list that describes and values each breed

[46] watchdog

[47] enclosed

[48] distinction

[49] general list

[50] rank

[51] strikes

[52] battered by

[53] risk

[54] hostility

[55] heart

[56] justify

[57] bewail

[58] beseech your help

[59] miscellaneous; various

100 As hounds and greyhounds, mongrels, spaniels, curs,[40]
Shoughs,[41] waterrugs,[42] and demi-wolves[43] are clept[44]
All by the name of dogs. The valued file[45]
Distinguishes the swift, the slow, the subtle,
The housekeeper,[46] the hunter, every one
105 According to the gift which bounteous nature
Hath in him closed,[47] whereby he does receive
Particular addition,[48] from the bill[49]
That writes them all alike; and so of men.
Now if you have a station[50] in the file,
110 Not i' the worst rank of manhood, say it,
And I will put that business in your bosoms,
Whose execution takes your enemy off,
Grapples you to the heart and love of us,
Who wear our health but sickly in his life,
115 Which in his death were perfect.
SECOND MURDERER: I am one, my liege,
Whom the vile blows and buffets[51] of the world
Have so incensed that I am reckless what
I do to spite the world.
120 FIRST MURDERER: And I another
So weary with disasters, tugg'd with[52] fortune,
That I would set[53] my life on any chance,
To mend it or be rid on 't.
MACBETH: Both of you
125 Know Banquo was your enemy.
BOTH MURDERERS: True, my lord.
MACBETH: So is he mine, and in such bloody distance[54]
That every minute of his being thrusts
Against my near'st of life:[55] and though I could
130 With barefaced power sweep him from my sight
And bid my will avouch[56] it, yet I must not,
For certain friends that are both his and mine,
Whose loves I may not drop, but wail[57] his fall
Who I myself struck down. And thence it is
135 That I to your assistance do make love,[58]
Masking the business from the common eye
For sundry[59] weighty reasons.
SECOND MURDERER: We shall, my lord,
Perform what you command us.

140 FIRST MURDERER: Though our lives—
    MACBETH: Your spirits shine through you. Within this hour at
        most
      I will advise you where to plant yourselves,
      Acquaint you with the perfect spy o' the time,[60]
145   The moment on 't;[61] for 't must be done tonight,
      And something[62] from the palace; always thought[63]
      That I require a clearness;[64] and with him—
      To leave no rubs[65] nor botches in the work—
      Fleance his son, that keeps him company,
150   Whose absence is no less material[66] to me
      Than is his father's, must embrace the fate
      Of that dark hour. Resolve[67] yourselves apart:[68]
      I'll come to you anon.
    BOTH MURDERERS: We are resolved, my lord.
155 MACBETH: I'll call upon you straight. Abide within.
      It is concluded: Banquo, thy soul's flight,
      If it find heaven, must find it out tonight.

Exeunt.

[60]*opportunity*

[61]*of it*

[62]*away*

[63]*remembering*

[64]*appearance of innocence*

[65]*flaws*

[66]*important*

[67]*make up your minds*

[68]*in private*

SCENE II
[The palace.]

Enter Macbeth's Lady, and a Servant.

LADY MACBETH: Is Banquo gone from court?
SERVANT: Ay, madam, but returns again tonight.
LADY MACBETH: Say to the King I would attend his leisure
    For a few words.
5 SERVANT: Madam, I will.   *[Exit.]*
LADY MACBETH: Nought's had, all's spent,
    Where our desire is got without content.[69]
    'Tis safer to be that which we destroy
    Than by destruction dwell in doubtful joy.

Enter Macbeth.
10   How now, my lord! Why do you keep alone,

[69]*happiness*

Of sorriest fancies your companions making,
Using those thoughts which should indeed have died
With them they think on?[70] Things without all remedy
Should be without regard. What's done is done.

15 MACBETH: We have scotch'd[71] the snake, not kill'd it.
She'll close[72] and be herself, whilst our poor malice
Remains in danger of her former tooth.[73]
But let the frame of things disjoint, both the worlds[74] suffer,
Ere we will eat our meal in fear and sleep
20 In the affliction of these terrible dreams
That shake us nightly. Better be with the dead,
Whom we, to gain our peace, have sent to peace,
Than on the torture of the mind to lie
In restless ecstasy.[75] Duncan is in his grave;
25 After life's fitful fever he sleeps well;
Treason has done his worst: nor steel, nor poison,
Malice domestic, foreign levy,[76] nothing,
Can touch him further.

LADY MACBETH: Come on,
30 Gentle my lord, sleek o'er your rugged looks;
Be bright and jovial among your guests tonight.

MACBETH: So shall I, love, and so, I pray, be you:
Let your remembrance[77] apply to Banquo;
Present him eminence,[78] both with eye and tongue:
35 Unsafe the while, that we
Must lave[79] our honors[80] in these flattering streams,
And make our faces vizards[81] to our hearts,
Disguising what they are.

LADY MACBETH: You must leave this.

40 MACBETH: O, full of scorpions is my mind, dear wife!
Thou know'st that Banquo and his Fleance lives.

LADY MACBETH: But in them nature's copy's[82] not eterne.[83]

MACBETH: There's comfort yet; they are assailable.
Then be thou jocund.[84] Ere the bat hath flown
45 His cloister'd[85] flight; ere to black Hecate's summons
The shard-borne[86] beetle with his drowsy hums
Hath rung night's yawning peal,[87] there shall be done
A deed of dreadful note.

LADY MACBETH: What's to be done?

50 MACBETH: Be innocent of the knowledge, dearest chuck,[88]

[handwritten:] poker face

[handwritten:] I wont tell you till you find out + you will applaud me

[70] about

[71] wounded

[72] heal

[73] fang [Snakes can still deliver venom after they have been killed.]

[74] heaven and earth

[75] madness

[76] army

[77] of how to behave

[78] honors

[79] wash

[80] reputations

[81] masks

[82] copyright, lease

[83] eternal

[84] cheerful

[85] covered in darkness†

[86] dung-born

[87] chime

[88] chick [a term of endearment]

Till thou applaud the deed. Come, seeling[89] night,

Scarf up[90] the tender eye of pitiful day,

And with thy bloody and invisible hand

Cancel and tear to pieces that great bond[91]

55   Which keeps me pale! Light thickens, and the crow

Makes wing to the rooky[92] wood:

Good things of day begin to droop and drowse,

Whiles night's black agents to their preys do rouse.

Thou marvell'st at my words, but hold thee still:

60   Things bad begun make strong themselves by ill.

So, prithee, go with me.

                                        Exeunt.

Lady was part of it before now she is not [handwritten annotation]

[89]*blinding*

[90]*blindfold*

[91]*i.e., Banquo's lease on life*

[92]*dark; the color of crows*

SCENE III

[A park near the palace.]

Enter three Murderers.

FIRST MURDERER: But who did bid thee join with us?

THIRD MURDERER: Macbeth.

SECOND MURDERER: He needs not our mistrust, since he delivers

5   Our offices[93] and what we have to do,

To the direction just.[94]

FIRST MURDERER: Then stand with us.

The west yet glimmers with some streaks of day;

Now spurs the lated[95] traveller apace

10   To gain the timely inn, and near approaches

The subject of our watch.

THIRD MURDERER: Hark! I hear horses.

BANQUO: *within.* Give us a light there, ho!

SECOND MURDERER: Then 'tis he: the rest

15   That are within the note of expectation[96]

Already are i' the court.

FIRST MURDERER: His horses go about.[97]

THIRD MURDERER: Almost a mile, but he does usually—

So all men do—from hence to the palace gate

20   Make it their walk.

[93]*instructions*

[94]*exactly*

[95]*belated*

[96]*list of expected guests*

[97]*have been turned out to pasture*

SECOND MURDERER: A light, a light!

Enter Banquo and Fleance, with a Torch.

THIRD MURDERER: 'Tis he.
FIRST MURDERER: Stand to't.
BANQUO: It will be rain tonight.
25 FIRST MURDERER: Let it come down.   *[They assault Banquo.]*
BANQUO: O, treachery! Fly, good Fleance, fly, fly, fly!
    Thou mayst revenge. O slave!
THIRD MURDERER: Who did strike out the light?
FIRST MURDERER: Was't not the way?
30 THIRD MURDERER: There's but one down; the son is fled.
SECOND MURDERER: We have lost best half of our affair.
FIRST MURDERER: Well, let's away and say how much is done.

                                                    Exeunt.

[handwritten: They only got one (killed) (banquo)]

SCENE IV
[In the palace.]

Banquet prepared. Enter Macbeth, Lady [Macbeth], Ross, Lennox, Lords, and Attendants.

MACBETH: You know your own degrees;[98] sit down. At first
    And last the hearty welcome.
LORDS: Thanks to your Majesty.
MACBETH: Ourself will mingle with society
5   And play the humble host.
    Our hostess keeps her state,[99] but in best time[100]
    We will require[101] her welcome.
LADY MACBETH: Pronounce it for me, sir, to all our friends,
    For my heart speaks they are welcome.

Enter first Murderer

10 MACBETH: See, they encounter[102] thee with their hearts' thanks.

[98] ranks (and thus seating locations)

[99] seated position on the throne

[100] good time

[101] request

[102] greet

Both sides are even: here I'll sit i' the midst:
Be large[103] in mirth; anon we'll drink a measure
The table round. There's blood upon thy face.

MURDERER: 'Tis Banquo's then.

15 MACBETH: 'Tis better thee without[104] than he within.[105]
Is he dispatch'd?

MURDERER: My lord, his throat is cut; that I did for him.

MACBETH: Thou art the best o' the cut-throats! Yet he's good
That did the like for Fleance. If thou didst it,

20 Thou art the nonpareil.[106]

MURDERER: Most royal sir,
Fleance is 'scaped.

MACBETH: Then comes my fit again: I had else been perfect,
Whole as the marble, founded[107] as the rock,

25 As broad and general[108] as the casing[109] air:
But now I am cabin'd, cribb'd,[110] confined, bound in
To saucy[111] doubts and fears.—But Banquo's safe? *dead*

MURDERER: Ay, my good lord. Safe in a ditch he bides,
With twenty trenched gashes on his head;

30 The least a death to nature.

MACBETH: Thanks for that.
There the grown serpent lies; the worm[112] that's fled
Hath nature that in time will venom breed,
No teeth for the present. Get thee gone. Tomorrow

35 We'll hear ourselves again.

Exit Murderer.

LADY MACBETH: My royal lord,
You do not give the cheer.[113] The feast is sold[114]
That is not often vouch'd, while 'tis a-making,

40 'Tis given with welcome.[115] To feed[116] were best at home;
From thence[117] the sauce to meat is ceremony;
Meeting were[118] bare without it.

MACBETH: Sweet remembrancer![119]
Now good digestion wait on appetite, *not paying attention to party*

45 And health on both!

LENNOX: May't please your Highness sit.

Enter Ghost of Banquo, and sits in Macbeth's place.

[103]*generous*

[104]*outside*

[105]*inside*

[106]*best; person without equal*

[107]*built solidly*

[108]*free*

[109]*surrounding*

[110]*cramped*

[111]*rude*

[112]*young serpent*

[113]*proper entertainment*

[114]*not given freely*

[115]*i.e., if the host is unfriendly*

[116]*merely eat*

[117]*home*

[118]*would be*

[119]*reminder*

[120]*nobility*

[121]*under one roof*

[122]*accuse of*

[123]*mishap; accident*

[124]*calls into question*

MACBETH: Here had we now our country's honor[120] roof'd,[121]
Were the graced person of our Banquo present;
50   Who may I rather challenge for[122] unkindness
Than pity for mischance![123]
ROSS: His absence, sir,
Lays blame upon[124] his promise. Please't your Highness
To grace us with your royal company?
55 MACBETH: The table's full.
LENNOX: Here is a place reserved, sir.
MACBETH: Where?
LENNOX: Here, my good lord. What is't that moves your
Highness?
60 MACBETH: Which of you have done this?
LORDS: What, my good lord?
MACBETH: Thou canst not say I did it: never shake
Thy gory locks at me. *don't shake your*
ROSS: Gentlemen, rise; his Highness is not well. *bloody*

has nothing to do with death

[125]*moment*

[126]*pay attention to*

[127]*aggravate*

[128]*strong emotion*

65 LADY MACBETH: Sit, worthy friends; my lord is often thus, *head*
And hath been from his youth. Pray you, keep seat. *at me*
The fit is momentary; upon a thought[125]
He will again be well. If much you note[126] him,
You shall offend him and extend[127] his passion:[128]
70   Feed, and regard him not. Are you a man?
MACBETH: Ay, and a bold one, that dare look on that
Which might appal the devil.

[129]*nonsense*

LADY MACBETH: O proper stuff![129]
This is the very painting of your fear;

[130]*floating*

[131]*outbursts*

[132]*weak imitations*

75   This is the air-drawn[130] dagger which, you said,
Led you to Duncan. O, these flaws[131] and starts,
Impostors[132] to true fear, would well become
A woman's story at a winter's fire,
Authorized by her grandam. Shame itself!
80   Why do you make such faces? When all's done,
You look but on a stool.
MACBETH: Prithee, see there! Behold! Look! Lo! How say
you?
Why, what care I? If thou canst nod, speak too.

[133]*tombs for the bones of the dead*

[134]*crypts*

[135]*stomachs*

[136]*birds of prey*

85   If charnel houses[133] and our graves must send
Those that we bury back, our monuments[134]
Shall be the maws[135] of kites.[136]   [*Exit Ghost.*]

LADY MACBETH: What, quite unmann'd in folly?

MACBETH: If I stand here, I saw him.

90 LADY MACBETH: Fie, for shame!

MACBETH: Blood hath been shed ere now, i' the olden time,

Ere humane statute[137] purged[138] the gentle weal;[139]

Ay, and since too, murders have been perform'd

Too terrible for the ear. The time has been,

95   That, when the brains were out, the man would die,

And there an end; but now they rise again,

With twenty mortal murders[140] on their crowns,[141]

And push us from our stools. This is more strange

Than such a murder is.

100 LADY MACBETH: My worthy lord,

Your noble friends do lack[142] you.

MACBETH: I do forget.

Do not muse at[143] me, my most worthy friends.

I have a strange infirmity, which is nothing

105   To those that know me. Come, love and health to all;

Then I'll sit down. Give me some wine, fill full.

Enter Ghost

I drink to the general joy o' the whole table,

And to our dear friend Banquo, whom we miss.

Would he were here! To all and him we thirst,

110   And all to all.

LORDS: Our duties and the pledge.[144]

MACBETH: Avaunt, and quit my sight! Let the earth hide thee!

Thy bones are marrowless, thy blood is cold;

Thou hast no speculation[145] in those eyes

115   Which thou dost glare with.

LADY MACBETH: Think of this, good peers,

But as a thing of custom. 'Tis no other,

Only it spoils the pleasure of the time.

MACBETH: What man dare, I dare.

120   Approach thou like the rugged Russian bear,

The arm'd[146] rhinoceros, or the Hyrcan[147] tiger;

Take any shape but that, and my firm nerves

Shall never tremble. Or be alive again,

And dare me to the desert[148] with thy sword.

125   If trembling I inhabit then, protest[149] me

[137]*law*

[138]*cleansed*

[139]*peaceful commonwealth*

[140]*fatal wounds*

[141]*heads*

[142]*miss*

[143]*worry about*

[144]*toast*

[145]*sight*

[146]*armored*

[147]*from a region near the Caspian Sea*

[148]*deserted place*

[149]*declare*

[150] *a baby girl*

[151] *amazing*

[152] *a stranger*

[153] *own*

[154] *drained of color*

[155] *stay*

[156] *the order in which each social rank is normally dismissed*

[157] *predictions of the future*†

[158] *connections among recent events*

[159] *magpies*

[160] *jackdaws (gray birds similar to crows)*

[161] *murderer*

[162] *time of night is it*

[163] *What do you think*

[164] *paid to spy*

[165] *soon*

[166] *determined*

   The baby of a girl.[150] Hence, horrible shadow!
   Unreal mockery, hence!   *[Exit Ghost.]*
   Why, so: being gone,
   I am a man again. Pray you, sit still.
130 LADY MACBETH: You have displaced the mirth, broke the
     good meeting,
   With most admired[151] disorder.
  MACBETH: Can such things be,
   And overcome us like a summer's cloud,
135 Without our special wonder? You make me strange[152]
   Even to the disposition that I owe,[153]
   When now I think you can behold such sights,
   And keep the natural ruby of your cheeks
   When mine is blanch'd[154] with fear.
140 ROSS: What sights, my lord?
  LADY MACBETH: I pray you, speak not; he grows worse and
     worse; *says hes sick*
   Question enrages him. At once, good night:
   Stand[155] not upon the order[156] of your going,
145 But go at once.
  LENNOX: Good night, and better health
   Attend his Majesty!
  LADY MACBETH: A kind good night to all!
             Exeunt Lords.
  MACBETH: It will have blood: they say blood will have blood.
150 Stones have been known to move and trees to speak;
   Augures[157] and understood relations[158] have
   By maggot pies[159] and choughs[160] and rooks brought forth
   The secret'st man of blood.[161] What is the night?[162]
  LADY MACBETH: Almost at odds with morning, which is
155   which. *suspects Macduff*
  MACBETH: How say'st thou,[163] that Macduff denies his person
   At our great bidding?
  LADY MACBETH: Did you send to him, sir?
  MACBETH: I hear it by the way, but I will send.
160 There's not a one of them but in his house
   I keep a servant fee'd.[164] I will tomorrow,
   And betimes[165] I will, to the weird sisters.
   More shall they speak; for now I am bent[166] to know,
   By the worst means, the worst. For mine own good

Macbeth is becoming unreasonable.

(handwritten top:) immoral→ amoral- NO moral code. (sociopaths) In opposing to your moral code

165   All causes[167] shall give way. I am in blood

       Stepp'd in so far that, should[168] I wade no more,

       Returning were[169] as tedious as go o'er.[170]

       Strange things I have in head that will to hand,[171]

       Which must be acted ere they may be scann'd.[172]

170 LADY MACBETH: You lack the season[173] of all natures, sleep.

       MACBETH: Come, we'll to sleep. My strange and self-abuse

       Is the initiate[174] fear that wants[175] hard use.[176]

       We are yet but young in deed.

                              Exeunt.

(handwritten right margin:) you need sleep

(handwritten:) hes killed so many, he cant go back / Thinking of bad things to do

SCENE V

[A heath.]

(handwritten:) Hecate - queen of the witches

Thunder. Enter the three Witches, meeting Hecate.

FIRST WITCH: Why, how now, Hecate? You look angerly.

HECATE: Have I not reason, beldams[177] as you are,

     Saucy and overbold? How did you dare

     To trade and traffic with Macbeth

5   In riddles and affairs of death;

     And I, the mistress of your charms,

     The close[178] contriver of all harms,

     Was never call'd to bear my part,

     Or show the glory of our art?

10   And, which is worse, all you have done

     Hath been but for a wayward son,

     Spiteful and wrathful: who, as others do,

     Loves for his own ends, not for you.

     But make amends now. Get you gone,

15   And at the pit of Acheron[179]

     Meet me i' the morning. Thither he

     Will come to know his destiny.

     Your vessels[180] and your spells provide,

     Your charms and every thing beside.

20   I am for the air; this night I'll spend[181]

     Unto a dismal and a fatal end.

[167] other issues

[168] if

[169] would be

[170] continuing to the other side

[171] be done

[172] fully contemplated

[173] preserving spice

[174] beginner's

[175] lacks

[176] experience

[177] hags

[178] secret

[179] river of hell

[180] cauldrons

[181] use

Great business must be wrought ere noon:
Upon the corner of the moon

[182]heavy

There hangs a vaporous drop profound;[182]
25 I'll catch it ere it come to ground.

[183]tricks

And that distill'd by magic sleights[183]

[184]deceitful

Shall raise such artificial[184] sprites. *fairies*
As by the strength of their illusion
Shall draw him on to his confusion.
30 He shall spurn fate, scorn death, and bear
His hopes 'bove wisdom, grace, and fear.

[185]overconfidence

And you all know security[185]
Is mortals' chiefest enemy.

Music, and a song.

Hark! I am call'd; my little spirit, see,
35 Sits in a foggy cloud and stays for me.

Sing within[:] Come away, Come away, etc.

FIRST WITCH: Come, let's make haste; she'll soon be back
again.   *Exeunt.*

Lennox's theory: Banquo was killed b/c he was out to late?

SCENE VI
[Forres. The palace.]

Enter Lennox, and another Lord.

[186]matched

LENNOX: My former speeches have but hit[186] your thoughts,

[187]deduce

Which can interpret[187] farther: only I say

[188]borne out

Things have been strangely borne.[188] The gracious Duncan

[189]by

Was pitied of[189] Macbeth: marry,[190] he was dead.

[190]indeed

5 And the right valiant Banquo walk'd too late,
Whom, you may say, if't please you, Fleance kill'd,
For Fleance fled. Men must not walk too late.

[191]help but think

Who cannot want the thought,[191] how monstrous
It was for Malcolm and for Donalbain

[192]deed

10 To kill their gracious father? Damned fact![192]

[193]immediately

How it did grieve Macbeth! Did he not straight,[193]
In pious rage, the two delinquents tear,

[194]captives

That were the slaves of drink and thralls[194] of sleep?
Was not that nobly done? Ay, and wisely too,

malcom + Donalbain in jeopardy:

15 For 'twould have anger'd any heart alive

To hear the men deny't. So that, I say,
He has borne all things well; and I do think
That, had he Duncan's sons under his key—
As, an't[195] please heaven, he shall not—they should find
20 What 'twere to kill a father; so should Fleance.
But, peace! For from broad words,[196] and 'cause he fail'd
His presence at the tyrant's feast, I hear,
Macduff lives in disgrace. Sir, can you tell
Where he bestows himself?
25 LORD: The son of Duncan,
From whom this tyrant holds[197] the due of birth,[198]
Lives in the English court and is received
Of the most pious Edward[199] with such grace
That the malevolence of fortune nothing
30 Takes[200] from his[201] high respect. Thither Macduff
Is gone to pray the holy King, upon his aid[202]
To wake Northumberland and warlike Siward;
That by the help of these, with Him above
To ratify[203] the work, we may again
35 Give to our tables meat, sleep to our nights,
Free from our feasts and banquets bloody knives,
Do faithful homage, and receive free[204] honors—
All which we pine for now. And this report
Hath so exasperate the King that he
40 Prepares for some attempt of war.
LENNOX: Sent he to Macduff?
LORD: He did: and with[205] an absolute "Sir, not I,"
The cloudy[206] messenger turns me his back,
And hums, as who should say, "You'll rue the time
45 That clogs[207] me with this answer."
LENNOX: And that well might
Advise him to a caution, to hold what distance
His wisdom can provide. Some holy angel
Fly to the court of England and unfold
50 His message ere he come, that a swift blessing
May soon return to this our suffering country
Under a hand accursed!
LORD: I'll send my prayers with him.

Exeunt.

[195]if it

[196]plain speaking

[197]withholds

[198]birthright

[199]King Edward, ruler of England 1042-1066

[200]detracts

[201]Malcolm's

[202]Malcolm's behalf

[203]condone

[204]without punishment

[205]after hearing

[206]scowling

[207]burdens

ACT IV

SCENE I
[A cavern. In the middle, a cauldron.]

Thunder. Enter the three Witches.

FIRST WITCH: Thrice the brinded[1] cat hath mew'd.
SECOND WITCH: Thrice and once the hedge-pig[2] whined.
THIRD WITCH: Harpier[3] cries, "'Tis time, 'tis time."
FIRST WITCH: Round about the cauldron go:
5   In the poison'd entrails throw.
     Toad, that under cold stone
     Days and nights has thirty-one
     Swelter'd[4] venom sleeping got,[5]
     Boil thou first i' the charmed pot.
10 ALL: Double, double, toil and trouble;
     Fire burn and cauldron bubble.
SECOND WITCH: Fillet[6] of a fenny[7] snake,
     In the cauldron boil and bake;
     Eye of newt and toe of frog,
15   Wool of bat and tongue of dog,
     Adder's fork[8] and blind-worm's[9] sting,
     Lizard's leg and howlet's[10] wing,
     For a charm of powerful trouble,
     Like a hell-broth boil and bubble.
20 ALL: Double, double, toil and trouble;
     Fire burn and cauldron bubble.
THIRD WITCH: Scale of dragon, tooth of wolf,
     Witch's mummy, maw[11] and gulf[12]
     Of the ravin'd[13] salt-sea shark,
25   Root of hemlock digg'd i' the dark,
     Liver of blaspheming Jew,
     Gall of goat and slips of yew

[1] striped
[2] hedgehog
[3] the third witch's familiar
[4] sweated
[5] formed while the toad slept
[6] slice
[7] swamp
[8] forked tongue
[9] a small, newt-like lizard once thought to be poisonous
[10] owlet
[11] stomach
[12] gullet
[13] ravenous

Witches at time were mad, felt that they were giving away one of their spells

¹⁴Cut off

Sliver'd[14] in the moon's eclipse,
Nose of Turk and Tartar's lips,

30   Finger of birth-strangled babe

¹⁵whore

Ditch-deliver'd by a drab,[15]

¹⁶viscous

Make the gruel thick and slab.[16]

¹⁷entrails

Add thereto a tiger's chaudron,[17]
For the ingredients of our cauldron.

35   ALL: Double, double, toil and trouble;
Fire burn and cauldron bubble.
SECOND WITCH: Cool it with a baboon's blood,
Then the charm is firm and good.

Enter Hecate, and the other three Witches.

HECATE: O, well done! I commend your pains,

40   And everyone shall share i' the gains.
And now about the cauldron sing,
Like elves and fairies in a ring,
Enchanting all that you put in.

Music and a song[:] Black spirits.

SECOND WITCH: By the pricking of my thumbs,

45 ✳ Something wicked this way comes:
Open, locks,
Whoever knocks!

Enter Macbeth.

MACBETH: How now, you secret, black, and midnight hags?
What is't you do?

50 ALL: A deed without a name.
MACBETH: I conjure you, by that which you profess,
Howe'er you come to know it, answer me:
Though you untie the winds and let them fight

¹⁸foamy

Against the churches, though the yeasty[18] waves

¹⁹unripe

55   Confound and swallow navigation up,

²⁰beaten down

Though bladed[19] corn be lodged[20] and trees blown down,

²¹guards'

Though castles topple on their warders'[21] heads,

²²let fall

Though palaces and pyramids do slope[22]

How come you know this info?

Their heads to their foundations, though the treasure
60 Of nature's germens[23] tumble all together
Even till destruction sicken,[24] answer me
To what I ask you.

FIRST WITCH: Speak.

SECOND WITCH: Demand.

65 THIRD WITCH: We'll answer.

FIRST WITCH: Say, if thou'dst rather hear it from our mouths,
or from our masters?

MACBETH: Call 'em, let me see 'em.

FIRST WITCH: Pour in sow's blood that hath eaten
70 Her nine farrow;[25] grease that's sweaten[26]
From the murderer's gibbet[27] throw
Into the flame.

ALL: Come, high or low;
Thyself and office[28] deftly show!

Thunder. First Apparition, an Armed Head.

75 MACBETH: Tell me, thou unknown power,—

FIRST WITCH: He knows thy thought:
Hear his speech, but say thou nought.

FIRST APPARITION: Macbeth! Macbeth! Macbeth! Beware
Macduff;
80 Beware the Thane of Fife. Dismiss me. Enough.

He descends.

MACBETH: Whate'er thou art, for thy good caution, thanks;
Thou hast harp'd[29] my fear aright. But one word more—

FIRST WITCH: He will not be commanded. Here's another,
More potent than the first.

Thunder. Second Apparition, a Bloody Child.

85 SECOND APPARITION: Macbeth! Macbeth! Macbeth!

SECOND APPARITION: Be bloody, bold, and resolute; laugh to
scorn
The power of man, for none of woman born
Shall harm Macbeth.

Descends.

90 MACBETH: Then live, Macduff. What need I fear of thee?
But yet I'll make assurance double sure,

[23]*seeds*

[24]*become too full*

[25]*offspring*

[26]*sweated*

[27]*gallows*†

[28]*purpose*

[29]*expressed, as one would play a note on a harp string*

[30]hold fate to its
   promise

And take a bond of fate:[30] thou shalt not live,
That I may tell pale-hearted fear it lies,
And sleep in spite of thunder.

*Thunder. Third Apparition; a Child Crowned, with a tree in his
hand.*

95   What is this,

[31]child

That rises like the issue[31] of a king,
And wears upon his baby brow the round

[32]i.e., the crown

And top[32] of sovereignty?
ALL: Listen, but speak not to't.

100   THIRD APPARITION: Be lion-mettled, proud, and take no care
Who chafes, who frets, or where conspirers are:
Macbeth shall never vanquish'd be until
Great Birnam Wood to high Dunsinane Hill
Shall come against him.   *Descends.*

105   MACBETH: That will never be.

[33]compel ⟶

Who can impress[33] the forest, bid the tree

[34]prophecies; omens

Unfix his earth-bound root? Sweet bodements,[34] good!
Rebellion's head, rise never, till the Wood
Of Birnam rise, and our high-placed Macbeth

[35]natural lifespan

110   Shall live the lease of nature,[35] pay his breath

[36]natural death

To time and mortal custom.[36] Yet my heart
Throbs to know one thing: tell me, if your art
Can tell so much, shall Banquo's issue ever
Reign in this kingdom?

*will will
banquos
children
be kings?.*

115   ALL: Seek to know no more.
MACBETH: I will be satisfied! Deny me this,
And an eternal curse fall on you! Let me know:
Why sinks that cauldron? and what noise is this?
                                                      Hautboys.

FIRST WITCH: Show!

120   SECOND WITCH: Show!
THIRD WITCH: Show!
ALL: Show his eyes, and grieve his heart;
Come like shadows, so depart!

[37]mirror

*A show of eight Kings, and Banquo last with a glass[37] in his
hand.*

MACBETH: Thou are too like the spirit of Banquo. Down!
125   Thy crown does sear mine eyeballs. And thy hair,
Thou other gold-bound brow, is like the first.
A third is like the former. Filthy hags!
Why do you show me this? A fourth! Start,[38] eyes!
What, will the line stretch out to the crack of doom?
130   Another yet! A seventh! I'll see no more:
And yet the eighth appears, who bears a glass
Which shows me many more; and some I see
That twofold balls[39] and treble[40] sceptres carry:
Horrible sight! Now I see 'tis true;
135   For the blood-bolter'd[41] Banquo smiles upon me,
And points at them for his. What, is this so?
FIRST WITCH: Ay, sir, all this is so. But why
Stands Macbeth thus amazedly?[42]
Come, sisters, cheer we up his sprites,[43]
140   And show the best of our delights.
I'll charm the air to give a sound,
While you perform your antic round,[44]
That this great King may kindly say
Our duties did his welcome pay.[45]

Music. The Witches dance, and vanish.

145 MACBETH: Where are they? Gone? Let this pernicious hour
Stand aye accursed in the calendar!
Come in, without there![46]

Enter Lennox.

LENNOX: What's your Grace's will?
MACBETH: Saw you the weird sisters?
150 LENNOX: No, my lord.
MACBETH: Came they not by you?
LENNOX: No indeed, my lord.
MACBETH: Infected be the air whereon they ride,
And damn'd all those that trust them! I did hear
155   The galloping of horse. Who was't came by?
LENNOX: 'Tis two or three, my lord, that bring you word
Macduff is fled to England.

[38]bulge out

[39]orbs representing England and Scotland

[40]triple (possibly England, Scotland, and Ireland)

[41]having hair matted with blood

[42]entranced

[43]spirits

[44]dance

[46]you outside

MACBETH: Fled to England? *already knew*

LENNOX: Ay, my good lord.

160   MACBETH: [*Aside.*] Time, thou anticipatest[47] my dread exploits.

     The flighty purpose[48] never is o'ertook[49]

     Unless the deed[50] go with it. From this moment

     The very firstlings[51] of my heart shall be

     The firstlings of my hand. And even now,

165   To crown my thoughts with acts, be it thought and done:

     The castle of Macduff I will surprise,

     Seize upon Fife; give to the edge o' the sword

     His wife, his babes, and all unfortunate souls

     That trace him in his line. No boasting like a fool;

170   This deed I'll do before this purpose cool. *See no*

     But no more sights!—Where are these gentlemen? *more*

     Come, bring me where they are. *appar*

                           Exeunt.

whatever he thinks with his brain, he will do with his hands.

he will kill everyone in Macduffs house

Macbeth is becoming more and more irrational.

SCENE II

[Fife. Macduff's castle.]

Enter Macduff's wife, her Son, and Ross.

LADY MACDUFF: What had he done, to make him fly the land?

ROSS: You must have patience, madam.

LADY MACDUFF: He had none;

     His flight was madness. When our actions do not,

5   Our fears do make us traitors.

ROSS: You know not

     Whether it was his wisdom or his fear.

LADY MACDUFF: Wisdom? To leave his wife, to leave his

         babes,

10   His mansion, and his titles,[52] in a place

     From whence himself does fly? He loves us not;

     He wants[53] the natural touch:[54] for the poor wren,

     The most diminutive of birds, will fight,

     Her young ones in her nest, against the owl.

15   All is the fear and nothing is the love;

[47]*hinder*

[48]*intention*

[49]*accomplished*

[50]*action*

[51]*first thoughts*

[52]*authority*

[53]*lacks*

[54]*protective instinct*

As little is the wisdom, where the flight
So runs against all reason.
Ross: My dearest coz,[55]
I pray you, school[56] yourself. But for your husband,
20   He is noble, wise, judicious, and best knows
The fits[57] o' the season.[58] I dare not speak much further;
But cruel are the times, when we are[59] traitors
And do not know ourselves;[60] when we hold[61] rumor
From[62] what we fear, yet know not what we fear,
25   But float upon a wild and violent sea
Each way and move. I take my leave of you;
Shall not be long but I'll be here again.
Things at the worst will cease, or else climb upward
To what they were before. My pretty cousin,
30   Blessing upon you!
Lady Macduff: Father'd he is, and yet he's fatherless.
Ross: I am so much a fool, should I stay longer,
It would be my disgrace and your discomfort.
I take my leave at once.   *Exit Ross.*
35   Lady Macduff: Sirrah, your father's dead.
And what will you do now? How will you live?
Son: As birds do, Mother.
Lady Macduff: What, with worms and flies?
Son: With what I get, I mean; and so do they.
40   Lady Macduff: Poor bird! Thou'ldst never fear the net nor
lime,[63]
The pitfall[64] nor the gin.[65]
Son: Why should I, Mother? Poor birds they[66] are not set for.
My father is not dead, for all your saying.
45   Lady Macduff: Yes, he is dead. How wilt thou do for a father?
Son: Nay, how will you do for a husband?
Lady Macduff: Why, I can buy me twenty at any market.
Son: Then you'll buy 'em to sell again.
Lady Macduff: Thou speak'st with all thy wit, and yet, i' faith,
50   With wit enough for thee.
Son: Was my father a traitor, Mother?
Lady Macduff: Ay, that he was.
Son: What is a traitor?
Lady Macduff: Why, one that swears and lies.[67]

[55]cousin

[56]control

[57]chaotic events

[58]present time

[59]are called

[60]know ourselves to be so

[61]believe

[62]based on

[63]birdlime, a sticky substance used to catch birds

[64]snare

[65]trap

[66]the traps

[67]breaks oaths

[handwritten annotation: Lady Macduff considers her husband dead for leaving]

55 SON: And be all traitors that do so?

LADY MACDUFF: Everyone that does so is a traitor and must be hanged.

SON: And must they all be hanged that swear and lie?

LADY MACDUFF: Every one.

60 SON: Who must hang them?

LADY MACDUFF: Why, the honest men.

SON: Then the liars and swearers are fools; for there are liars and swearers enough to beat the honest men and hang up them.

65 LADY MACDUFF: Now, God help thee, poor monkey! But how wilt thou do for a father?

SON: If he were dead, you'd weep for him: if you would not, it were a good sign that I should quickly have a new father.

70 LADY MACDUFF: Poor prattler, how thou talk'st!

Enter a Messenger.

[68]*regarding*
[69]*knowledgeable*
[70]*fear*
[71]*plain, unattractive*
[72]*brutal*
[73]*near*

MESSENGER: Bless you, fair dame! I am not to you known,
Though, in[68] your state of honor I am perfect.[69]
I doubt[70] some danger does approach you nearly.
If you will take a homely[71] man's advice,
75 Be not found here; hence, with your little ones.
To fright you thus, methinks I am too savage;
To do worse to you were fell[72] cruelty,
Which is too nigh[73] your person. Heaven preserve you!
I dare abide no longer.

80 LADY MACDUFF: Whither should I fly?
I have done no harm. But I remember now
I am in this earthly world, where to do harm
Is often laudable, to do good sometime

[74]*interpreted as*

Accounted[74] dangerous folly. Why then, alas,
85 Do I put up that womanly defense,
To say I have done no harm?—What are these faces?

Enter Murderers.

FIRST MURDERER: Where is your husband?

LADY MACDUFF: I hope, in no place so unsanctified

Where such as thou mayst find him.

FIRST MURDERER: He's a traitor.

90   SON: Thou liest, thou shag-ear'd villain!

FIRST MURDERER: What, you egg! [Stabs him.]

Young fry[75] of treachery!

SON: He has kill'd me, Mother.

Run away, I pray you!

Exit [Lady Macduff], crying "Murder!"

[Exeunt murderers.]

SCENE III

[England. Before the King's palace.]

Enter Malcolm and Macduff.= (ome from scotland

MALCOLM: Let us seek out some desolate shade and there
   Weep our sad bosoms empty.

MACDUFF: Let us rather
   Hold fast the mortal[76] sword, and like good men

5   Bestride[77] our downfall'n birthdom.[78] Each new morn
   New widows howl, new orphans cry, new sorrows
   Strike heaven on the face, that it resounds
   As if it felt with Scotland and yell'd out
   Like syllable of dolor.[79]

10   MALCOLM: What I believe, I'll wail;
   What know, believe; and what I can redress,[80]
   As I shall find the time to friend,[81] I will.
   What you have spoke, it may be so perchance.
   This tyrant, whose sole[82] name blisters our tongues,

15   Was once thought honest. You have loved him well;
   He hath not touch'd you yet. I am young, but something
   You may deserve of[83] him through[84] me, and wisdom[85]
   To offer up a weak, poor, innocent lamb
   To appease an angry god.

20   MACDUFF: I am not treacherous.

MALCOLM: But Macbeth is.
   A good and virtuous nature may recoil[86]

Macbeth
you haven't been hurt

[75]*offspring*

[76]*deadly*

[77]*Defend (as one would a wounded comrade)*

[78]*homeland*

[79]*pain*

[80]*correct*

[81]*opportune*

[82]*mere*

[83]*gain from*

[84]*by betraying*

[85]*it would be wise in that situation*

[86]*draw back, weaken*

[87]*royal order*

[88]*change*

[89]*Lucifer*

[90]*unprotected state*

[91]*suspicions*

[92]*safeguards*

[93]*perfectly honorable*

[94]*foundation*

[95]*ill-gotten gains*

[96]*confirmed*

[97]*as well*

[98]*distrust*

[99]*the king of England*

[100]*various types*

[101]*boundless*

In an imperial charge.[87] But I shall crave your pardon;
That which you are, my thoughts cannot transpose.[88]
25   Angels are bright still, though the brightest[89] fell.
Though all things foul would wear the brows of grace,
Yet grace must still look so.
MACDUFF: I have lost my hopes.
MALCOLM: Perchance even there where I did find my doubts.
30   Why in that rawness[90] left you wife and child,
Those precious motives, those strong knots of love,
Without leave-taking? I pray you,
Let not my jealousies[91] be your dishonors,
But mine own safeties.[92] You may be rightly just,[93]
35   Whatever I shall think.
MACDUFF: Bleed, bleed, poor country!
Great tyranny, lay thou thy basis[94] sure,
For goodness dare not check thee. Wear thou thy wrongs;[95]
The title is affeer'd.[96] Fare thee well, lord.
40   I would not be the villain that thou think'st
For the whole space that's in the tyrant's grasp
And the rich East to boot.[97]
MALCOLM: Be not offended;
I speak not as in absolute fear[98] of you.
45   I think our country sinks beneath the yoke;
It weeps, it bleeds, and each new day a gash
Is added to her wounds. I think withal
There would be hands uplifted in my right;
And here from gracious England[99] have I offer
50   Of goodly thousands. But for all this,
When I shall tread upon the tyrant's head,
Or wear it on my sword, yet my poor country
Shall have more vices than it had before,
More suffer and more sundry ways than ever,
55   By him that shall succeed.
MACDUFF: What should he be?
MALCOLM: It is myself I mean, in whom I know
All the particulars[100] of vice so grafted
That, when they shall be open'd, black Macbeth
60   Will seem as pure as snow, and the poor state
Esteem him as a lamb, being compared
With my confineless[101] harms.

MACDUFF: Not in the legions
 Of horrid hell can come a devil more damn'd
65 In evils to top Macbeth.
 MALCOLM: I grant him bloody,
 Luxurious,[102] avaricious, false, deceitful,
 Sudden,[103] malicious, smacking of every sin
 That has a name. But there's no bottom, none,
70 In my voluptuousness. Your wives, your daughters,
 Your matrons, and your maids could not fill up
 The cistern of my lust, and my desire
 All continent[104] impediments would o'erbear
 That did oppose my will. Better Macbeth
75 Than such an one to reign.
 MACDUFF: Boundless intemperance
 In nature[105] is a tyranny; it hath been
 The untimely emptying of the happy throne,
 And fall of many kings. But fear not yet
80 To take upon you what is yours. You may
 Convey[106] your pleasures in a spacious plenty[107]
 And yet seem cold,[108] the time you may so hoodwink.[109]
 We have willing dames enough; there cannot be
 That vulture in you, to devour so many
85 As will to greatness dedicate themselves,
 Finding it so inclined.
 MALCOLM: With this there grows
 In my most ill-composed affection[110] such
 A stanchless[111] avarice that, were I King,
90 I should cut off the nobles for their lands,
 Desire his jewels and this other's house,
 And my more-having would be as a sauce
 To make me hunger more, that I should forge
 Quarrels unjust against the good and loyal,
95 Destroying them for wealth.
 MACDUFF: This avarice
 Sticks deeper, grows with more pernicious root
 Than summer-seeming[112] lust, and it hath been
 The sword[113] of our slain kings. Yet do not fear;
100 Scotland hath foisons[114] to fill up your will[115]
 Of your mere own.[116] All these are portable,[117]
 With other graces weigh'd.

[102]*lecherous*

[103]*violent*

[104]*containing; confining*

[105]*human nature*

[106]*carry out*

[107]*great number*

[108]*chaste*

[109]*deceive*

[110]*nature*

[111]*insatiable*

[112]*youthful*

[113]*downfall*

[114]*plenty*

[115]*greed*

[116]*from your own royal assets*

[117]*tolerable*

MALCOLM: But I have none. The king-becoming graces,

As justice, verity, temperance, stableness,

[118]humility   105   Bounty, perseverance, mercy, lowliness,[118]

Devotion, patience, courage, fortitude,

[119]trace   I have no relish[119] of them, but abound

[120]separate   In the division of each several[120] crime,

Acting it many ways. Nay, had I power, I should

[121]harmony   110   Pour the sweet milk of concord[121] into hell,

Uproar the universal peace, confound

All unity on earth.

MACDUFF: O Scotland, Scotland!

MALCOLM: If such a one be fit to govern, speak.

115   I am as I have spoken.

MACDUFF: Fit to govern?

No, not to live. O nation miserable!

[122]illegitimate   With an untitled[122] tyrant bloody-scepter'd,

When shalt thou see thy wholesome days again,

[123]exclusion   120   Since that the truest issue of thy throne

[124]name   By his own interdiction[123] stands accursed,

And does blaspheme his breed?[124] Thy royal father

[125]on her knees in prayer   Was a most sainted king: the queen that bore thee,

Oftener upon her knees[125] than on her feet,

[126]was dead to the world   125   Died[126] every day she lived. Fare thee well!

These evils thou repeat'st upon thyself

Have banish'd me from Scotland. O my breast,

Thy hope ends here!

[127]display   MALCOLM: Macduff, this noble passion,[127]

130   Child of integrity, hath from my soul

[128]suspicions   Wiped the black scruples,[128] reconciled my thoughts

To thy good truth and honor. Devilish Macbeth

[129]schemes   By many of these trains[129] hath sought to win me

[130]prudence   Into his power, and modest wisdom[130] plucks me

135   From over-credulous haste. But God above

Deal between thee and me! For even now

I put myself to thy direction and

[131]retract   Unspeak[131] mine own detraction; here abjure

The taints and blames I laid upon myself,

140   For strangers to my nature. I am yet

[132]dishonest   Unknown to woman, never was forsworn,[132]

Scarcely have coveted what was mine own,

At no time broke my faith, would not betray
The devil to his fellow, and delight

145   No less in truth than life. My first false speaking
Was this upon myself. What I am truly,
Is thine and my poor country's to command:
Whither indeed, before thy here-approach,
Old Siward, with ten thousand warlike men,

150   Already at a point,[133] was setting forth.
Now we'll together, and the chance of goodness[134]
Be like[135] our warranted quarrel![136] Why are you silent?

MACDUFF: Such welcome and unwelcome things at once
'Tis hard to reconcile.

Enter a Doctor.

155   MALCOLM: Well, more anon. Comes the King forth, I pray
you?
DOCTOR: Ay, sir, there are a crew of wretched souls
That stay[137] his cure. Their malady convinces[138]
The great assay of art,[139] but at his touch,

160   Such sanctity hath heaven given his hand,
They presently amend.[140]
MALCOLM: I thank you, Doctor.   *Exit.*
MACDUFF: What's the disease he means?
MALCOLM: 'Tis call'd the evil:[141]

165   A most miraculous work in this good King,
Which often, since my here-remain in England,
I have seen him do. How he solicits[142] heaven,
Himself best knows; but strangely-visited[143] people,
All swol'n and ulcerous, pitiful to the eye,

170   The mere[144] despair of surgery, he cures,
Hanging a golden stamp[145] about their necks,
Put on with holy prayers: and 'tis spoken,
To the succeeding royalty he leaves
The healing benediction. With this strange virtue

175   He hath a heavenly gift of prophecy,
And sundry blessings hang about his throne
That speak him full of grace.

Enter Ross.

[133]prepared for
battle

[134]success

[135]equal to

[136]cause

[137]wait

[138]eludes

[139]efforts of medical
science

[140]heal

[141]The disease
scrofula, sometimes
called "The King's
Evil," was a form
of tuberculosis
thought to be cured
by a king's touch.

[142]petitions the
powers of

[143]afflicted

[144]utter

[145]coin

MACDUFF: See, who comes here?

MALCOLM: My countryman: but yet I know him not.

MACDUFF: My ever gentle cousin, welcome hither.

180 MALCOLM: I know him now. Good God, betimes[146] remove
    The means that makes us strangers!

ROSS: Sir, amen.

MACDUFF: Stands Scotland where it did?

ROSS: Alas, poor country,

185   Almost afraid to know itself! It cannot
    Be call'd our mother, but our grave. Where nothing,
    But who[147] knows nothing, is once seen to smile;
    Where sighs and groans and shrieks that rend the air,
    Are made, not mark'd;[148] where violent sorrow seems

190   A modern[149] ecstasy. The dead man's knell
    Is there scarce ask'd for who, and good men's lives
    Expire before the flowers in their caps,
    Dying or ere they sicken.

MACDUFF: O, relation[150]

195   Too nice,[151] and yet too true!

MALCOLM: What's the newest grief?

ROSS: That of an hour's age doth hiss the speaker;[152]
    Each minute teems a new one.

MACDUFF: How does my wife?

200 ROSS: Why, well.

MACDUFF: And all my children?

ROSS: Well too.

MACDUFF: The tyrant has not batter'd at their peace?

ROSS: No; they were well at peace when I did leave 'em.

205 MACDUFF: Be not a niggard[153] of your speech. How goes't?

ROSS: When I came hither to transport the tidings,
    Which I have heavily borne, there ran a rumor
    Of many worthy fellows that were out,[154]
    Which was to my belief witness'd the rather,[155]

210   For that[156] I saw the tyrant's power[157] a-foot:
    Now is the time of help; your eye in Scotland
    Would create soldiers, make our women fight,
    To doff[158] their dire distresses.

MALCOLM: Be't their comfort

215   We are coming thither. Gracious England hath
    Lent us good Siward and ten thousand men;

[146]quickly
[147]the one who
[148]noticed
[149]typical
[150]report
[151]accurate
[152]News an hour old gets hissed at for being too old
[153]miser
[154]armed
[155]made more believable
[156]because
[157]army
[158]cast off

An older[159] and a better soldier none[160]
That Christendom gives out.

[159]*more experienced*

[160]*there is none*

Ross: Would I could answer
220   This comfort with the like! But I have words
That would be howl'd out in the desert air,
Where hearing should not latch[161] them.

[161]*catch*

Macduff: What concern they?
The general cause? Or is it a fee-grief[162]
225   Due to[163] some single breast?

[162]*personal woe*

[163]*belonging to*

Ross: No mind that's honest
But in it shares some woe, though the main part
Pertains to you alone.

Macduff: If it be mine,
230   Keep it not from me, quickly let me have it.

Ross: Let not your ears despise my tongue for ever,
Which shall possess them with the heaviest sound
That ever yet they heard.

Macduff: Humh! I guess at it.
235 Ross: Your castle is surprised; your wife and babes
Savagely slaughter'd. To relate the manner
Were, on the quarry[164] of these murder'd deer,
To add the death of you.

[164]*heap*

Malcolm: Merciful heaven!
240   What, man! Ne'er pull your hat upon your brows;[165]
Give sorrow words. The grief that does not speak
Whispers the o'er fraught[166] heart, and bids it break.

[165]*conceal your
sorrow*

[166]*overburdened*

Macduff: My children too?

Ross: Wife, children, servants, all
245   That could be found.

Macduff: And I must be from thence!
My wife kill'd too?

Ross: I have said.

Malcolm: Be comforted.
250   Let's make us medicines of our great revenge,
To cure this deadly grief.

Macduff: He has no children. All my pretty ones?
Did you say all? O hell-kite! All?
What, all my pretty chickens and their dam
255   At one fell swoop?

Malcolm: Dispute it like a man.

[handwritten annotations: "Macbeth killed his family"; "use your grief to get back at Macbeth"; "I was not there to save them"; "get revenge"]

MACDUFF: I shall do so;
But I must also feel it as a man.
I cannot but remember such things were,
260   That were most precious to me. Did heaven look on,
And would not take their part? Sinful Macduff,
They were all struck for thee! Naught[167] that I am,
Not for their own demerits, but for mine,
Fell slaughter on their souls. Heaven rest them now!
265   MALCOLM: Be this the whetstone of your sword. Let grief
Convert to anger; blunt not the heart, enrage it.
MACDUFF: O, I could play the woman with mine eyes,
And braggart with my tongue! But, gentle heavens,
Cut short all intermission;[168] front to front[169]
270   Bring thou this fiend of Scotland and myself;
Within my sword's length set him; if he 'scape,
Heaven forgive him too!
MALCOLM: This tune goes manly.
Come, go we to the King; our power[170] is ready;
275   Our lack[171] is nothing but our leave.[172] Macbeth
Is ripe for shaking, and the powers above
Put on their instruments.[173] Receive what cheer you may;
The night is long that never finds the day.

                                                                                  Exeunt.

[167]*wicked person*

[168]*delay*

[169]*face to face*

[170]*army*

[171]*what remains*

[172]*departure*

[173]*prepare to help us in arms*

[handwritten margin notes:]
killed b/c of me
sharpen up
Macbeth
make him fight from fear
They want Macbeth to fall
Uless w/ Macbeth, nl will fall.

ACT V

SCENE I

[Dunsinane. Anteroom in the castle.]

Enter a Doctor of Physic, and a Waiting Gentlewoman.

DOCTOR: I have two nights watched[1] with you, but can perceive
no truth in your report. When was it she last walked?

GENTLEWOMAN: Since his Majesty went into the field, I have
seen her rise from her bed, throw her nightgown upon her,

5   unlock her closet, take forth paper, fold it, write upon't,
read it, afterwards seal it, and again return to bed; yet all
this while in a most fast sleep.

DOCTOR: A great perturbation in nature, to receive at once
the benefit of sleep and do the effects of watching! In this

10   slumbery agitation, besides her walking and other actual
performances, what, at any time, have you heard her say?

GENTLEWOMAN: That, sir, which I will not report after her.

DOCTOR: You may to me, and 'tis most meet[2] you should.

GENTLEWOMAN: Neither to you nor any one, having no witness

15   to confirm my speech.

Enter Lady [Macbeth], with a taper.[3]

Lo you, here she comes! This is her very guise,[4] and, upon
my life, fast asleep. Observe her; stand close.

DOCTOR: How came she by that light?

GENTLEWOMAN: Why, it stood by her. She has light by her con-

20   tinually; 'tis her command.

DOCTOR: You see, her eyes are open.

GENTLEWOMAN: Ay, but their sense is shut.

DOCTOR: What is it she does now? Look how she rubs her
hands.

[1]*stayed up*

[2]*proper*

[3]*candle*

[4]*usual routine*

75

25 GENTLEWOMAN: It is an accustomed action with her, to seem thus washing her hands. I have known her continue in this a quarter of an hour.

LADY MACBETH: Yet here's a spot.

DOCTOR: Hark, she speaks! I will set down what comes from

30 her, to satisfy my remembrance the more strongly.

LADY MACBETH: Out, damned spot! Out, I say! One—two-- why then 'tis time to do't. Hell is murky. Fie, my lord, fie! A soldier, and afeard? What need we fear who knows it, when none can call our power to account? Yet who would

35 have thought the old man to have had so much blood in him? *Duncan*

DOCTOR: Do you mark that? *Macduff*

LADY MACBETH: The Thane of Fife had a wife; where is she now? What, will these hands ne'er be clean? No more

40 o' that, my lord, no more o' that. You mar all with this starting. *heard what you should*

DOCTOR: Go to,[5] go to; you have known what you should not. *have not*

GENTLEWOMAN: She has spoke what she should not, I am sure of that. Heaven knows what she has known.

45 LADY MACBETH: Here's the smell of the blood still. All the perfumes of Arabia will not sweeten this little hand. Oh, oh, oh! *burdened w/ guilt*

DOCTOR: What a sigh is there! The heart is sorely charged.[6]

GENTLEWOMAN: I would not have such a heart in my bosom

50 for the dignity[7] of the whole body.

DOCTOR: Well, well, well—

GENTLEWOMAN: Pray God it be, sir. *I cannot do*

DOCTOR: This disease is beyond my practice.[8] Yet I have *any* known those which have walked in their sleep who have *thing*

55 died holily in their beds.

LADY MACBETH: Wash your hands, put on your nightgown; look not so pale. I tell you yet again, Banquo's buried; he cannot come out on's[9] grave.

DOCTOR: Even so? *porter*

60 LADY MACBETH: To bed, to bed; there's knocking at the gate. Come, come, come, come, give me your hand. What's done cannot be undone. To bed, to bed, to bed. *Macbeth kind*

               Exit Lady.

DOCTOR: Will she go now to bed?

[5]Shame

[6]burdened

[7]worth

[8]expertise

[9]of his

GENTLEWOMAN: Directly.

65 DOCTOR: Foul whisperings are abroad. Unnatural deeds
    Do breed unnatural troubles: infected minds
    To their deaf pillows will discharge their secrets:
    More needs she the divine[10] than the physician.
    God, God, forgive us all! Look after her;
70   Remove from her the means of all annoyance,[11]
    And still keep eyes upon her. So good night:
    My mind she has mated,[12] and amazed my sight:
    I think, but dare not speak.

GENTLEWOMAN: Good night, good doctor.

Exeunt.

[10]*priest*

[11]*self-injury*

[12]*bewildered*

[handwritten annotations: "has an infected mind", "needs god more than a physician", "keep her away from anything that could hurt her — suicide watch", "think — he knows whats wrong but wont dare say what it is."]

SCENE II

[The country near Dunsinane.]

Drum and colors. Enter Menteith, Caithness, Angus, Lennox,
[and] *Soldiers.* *[handwritten: "Getting ready for war"]*

MENTEITH: The English power is near, led on by Malcolm,
    His uncle Siward, and the good Macduff.
    Revenges burn in them, for their dear causes
    Would to the bleeding[13] and the grim[14] alarm[15]
5   Excite the mortified[16] man.

ANGUS: Near Birnam Wood
    Shall we well meet them; that way are they coming.

CAITHNESS: Who knows if Donalbain be with his brother?

LENNOX: For certain, sir, he is not; I have a file[17]
10   Of all the gentry.[18] There is Siward's son
    And many unrough[19] youths, that even now
    Protest[20] their first[21] of manhood.

MENTEITH: What does the tyrant?

CAITHNESS: Great Dunsinane he strongly fortifies.
15   Some say he's mad; others, that lesser hate him,
    Do call it valiant fury: but, for certain,
    He cannot buckle his distemper'd[22] cause
    Within the belt of rule.

ANGUS: Now does he feel

[13]*bloody*

[14]*desperate*

[15]*call to battle*

[16]*dead*

[17]*list*

[18]*members of the upper class*

[19]*beardless*

[20]*declare*

[21]*first rites (initiation into)*

[22]*swollen (from disease)*

[handwritten annotations: "revenge against Macbeth", "Macbeth", "his own men say he's crazy."]

20   His secret murders sticking on his hands,

[23 each minute]

Now minutely[23] revolts upbraid his faith-breach;

Those he commands move only in command,

Nothing in love. Now does he feel his title

Hang loose about him, like a giant's robe

25   Upon a dwarfish thief.

MENTEITH: Who then shall blame

[24 flinch]

His pester'd senses to recoil and start,[24]

When all that is within him does condemn

Itself for being there?

30   CAITHNESS: Well, march we on,

[25 i.e., Malcolm]

To give obedience where 'tis truly owed.

[26 state]

Meet we the medicine[25] of the sickly weal,[26]

And with him pour we, in our country's purge,

Each drop of us.

35   LENNOX: Or so much as it needs

To dew the sovereign flower and drown the weeds.

Make we our march towards Birnam.

Exeunt marching.

SCENE III

[Dunsinane. A room in the castle.]

Enter Macbeth, Doctor, and Attendants.

[27 the deserting
thanes]

MACBETH: Bring me no more reports; let them[27] fly all!

Till Birnam Wood remove to Dunsinane

I cannot taint with fear. What's the boy Malcolm?

Was he not born of woman? The spirits that know

5   All mortal consequences have pronounced me thus:

"Fear not, Macbeth; no man that's born of woman

Shall e'er have power upon thee." Then fly, false thanes,

[28 lovers of fine food
and drink]

And mingle with the English epicures![28]

The mind I sway by and the heart I bear

10   Shall never sag with doubt nor shake with fear.

Enter a Servant.

The devil damn thee black, thou cream-faced loon![29]
　Where got'st thou that goose look?
SERVANT: There is ten thousand—
MACBETH: Geese, villain?
15 SERVANT: Soldiers, sir.
MACBETH: Go prick thy face and over-red[30] thy fear,[31]
　Thou lily-liver'd[32] boy. What soldiers, patch?[33]
　Death of thy soul! Those linen cheeks of thine
　Are counselors to[34] fear. What soldiers, whey-face?
20 SERVANT: The English force, so please you.
MACBETH: Take thy face hence.
　Seyton—I am sick at heart,
　When I behold—Seyton, I say!—This push[35]
　Will cheer me ever or disseat[36] me now.
25 I have lived long enough. My way of life
　Is fall'n into the sear,[37] the yellow leaf,
　And that which should accompany old age,
　As honor, love, obedience, troops of friends,
　I must not look to have; but, in their stead,
30 Curses, not loud but deep, mouth-honor,[38] breath,
　Which the poor heart would fain deny and dare not.
　Seyton!

Enter Seyton.

SEYTON: What's your gracious pleasure?
MACBETH: What news more?
35 SEYTON: All is confirm'd, my lord, which was reported.
MACBETH: I'll fight, 'til from my bones my flesh be hack'd.
　Give me my armor.
SEYTON: 'Tis not needed yet.
MACBETH: I'll put it on.
40 Send out more horses, skirr[39] the country round,
　Hang those that talk of fear. Give me mine armor.
　How does your patient, doctor?
DOCTOR: Not so sick, my lord,
　As she is troubled with thick-coming fancies,
45 That keep her from her rest.
MACBETH: Cure her of that.
　Canst thou not minister to a mind diseased,

[29] fool
[30] make red
[31] fearful paleness
[32] white- (bloodless) livered [The liver was thought to be the source of courage.]
[33] fool
[34] teachers of
[35] impending battle
[36] dethrone
[37] withered and dry
[38] words said but not meant
[39] scour

[40] *causing memory loss*

          Pluck from the memory a rooted sorrow,
          Raze out the written troubles of the brain,
50   And with some sweet oblivious[40] antidote
          Cleanse the stuff'd bosom of that perilous stuff
          Which weighs upon the heart?
      DOCTOR: Therein the patient
          Must minister to himself.

[41] *medicine*

[42] *lance*

55 MACBETH: Throw physic[41] to the dogs, I'll none of it.
          Come, put mine armor on; give me my staff.[42]
          Seyton, send out. Doctor, the thanes fly from me.
          Come, sir, dispatch.[43] If thou couldst, doctor, cast

[43] *hurry*

[44] *test the urine*

          The water[44] of my land, find her disease
60   And purge it to a sound and pristine health,
          I would applaud thee to the very echo,
          That should applaud again. Pull't[45] off, I say.

[45] *pull it (an extra piece of armor)*

[46] *an herb used as a laxative*

          What rhubarb, senna,[46] or what purgative[47] drug
          Would scour these English hence? Hear'st thou of them?
65 DOCTOR: Ay, my good lord: your royal preparation

[47] *cleansing*

          Makes us hear something.
      MACBETH: Bring it after me.
          I will not be afraid of death and bane[48]

[48] *destruction*

          Till Birnam Forest come to Dunsinane.
70 DOCTOR: Were I from Dunsinane away and clear,
          Profit again[49] should hardly draw me here.

[49] *not even a large profit*

                                Exeunt.

SCENE IV
[Country near **Birnam Wood**.]

Drum and colors. Enter Malcolm, Siward, Macduff, Siward's son, Menteith, Caithness, Angus, and Soldiers marching.

MALCOLM: Cousins, I hope the days are near at hand
          That chambers[50] will be safe.
MENTEITH: We doubt it nothing.[51]
SIWARD: What wood is this before us?
5 MENTEITH: The Wood of Birnam.

[50] *bedrooms*

[51] *not at all*

MALCOLM: Let every soldier hew him down a bough,
     And bear't before him: thereby shall we shadow
     The numbers of our host,[52] and make discovery[53]
     Err in report of us.

10   SOLDIERS: It shall be done.

     SIWARD: We learn no other but the confident tyrant
     Keeps still in Dunsinane, and will endure
     Our setting down[54] before't.

     MALCOLM: 'Tis his main hope;

15   For where there is advantage to be given,
     Both more[55] and less[56] have given him the revolt,
     And none serve with him but constrained things
     Whose hearts are absent too.

     MACDUFF: Let our just censures[57]

20   Attend[58] the true[59] event, and put we on
     Industrious soldiership.

     SIWARD: The time approaches
     That will with due decision make us know
     What we shall say we have and what we owe.[60]

25   Thoughts speculative their unsure hopes relate,
     But certain issue[61] strokes[62] must arbitrate;[63]
     Towards which, advance the war.

                              Exeunt Marching.

[52]*forces*
[53]*enemy scouts*
[54]*siege*
[55]*rich*
[56]*poor*
[57]*hopes*
[58]*await*
[59]*actual*
[60]*own*
[61]*the actual outcome*
[62]*physical warfare*
[63]*decide*

SCENE V

[Dunsinane. Within the castle.]

Enter Macbeth, Seyton, and Soldiers, with drum and colors.

MACBETH: Hang out our banners on the outward walls;
     The cry is still, "They come": Our castle's strength
     Will laugh a siege to scorn. Here let them lie
     Till famine and the ague[64] eat them up.
     Were they not forced[65] with those that should be ours,
     We might have met them dareful, beard to beard,
     And beat them backward home.

                         A cry within of women.

     What is that noise?

[64]*disease*
[65]*reinforced*

SEYTON: It is the cry of women, my good lord.

10 MACBETH: I have almost forgot the taste of fears:

[66]*chilled with fear*

    The time has been, my senses would have cool'd[66]

    To hear a night-shriek, and my fell of hair

[67]*tale*

    Would at a dismal treatise[67] rouse and stir

    As life were in't: I have supp'd full with horrors;

    Direness, familiar to my slaughterous thoughts,

[68]*startle*

    Cannot once start[68] me.

    Wherefore was that cry?

SEYTON: The Queen, my lord, is dead.

MACBETH: She should have died hereafter;

20   There would have been a time for such a word.

    Tomorrow, and tomorrow, and tomorrow

    Creeps in this petty pace from day to day

    To the last syllable of recorded time;

    And all our yesterdays have lighted fools

25   The way to dusty death. Out, out, brief candle!

    Life's but a walking shadow, a poor player

    That struts and frets his hour upon the stage

    And then is heard no more. It is a tale

    Told by an idiot, full of sound and fury,

30   Signifying nothing.

Enter a Messenger.

    Thou comest to use thy tongue; thy story quickly.

MESSENGER: Gracious my lord,

    I should report that which I say I saw,

    But know not how to do it.

35 MACBETH: Well, say, sir.

MESSENGER: As I did stand my watch upon the hill,

    I look'd toward Birnam, and anon, methought,

    The Wood began to move.

MACBETH: Liar and slave!

40 MESSENGER: Let me endure your wrath, if't be not so.

    Within this three mile may you see it coming;

    I say, a moving grove.

MACBETH: If thou speak'st false,

    Upon the next tree shalt thou hang alive,

[69]*wither*

45   Till famine cling[69] thee; if thy speech be sooth,[70]

[70]*true*

    I care not if thou dost for me as much.

I pull[71] in resolution and begin   *doubts the*
To doubt the equivocation of the fiend   *witches now*
That lies like truth. "Fear not, till Birnam Wood
50   Do come to Dunsinane," and now a wood
Comes toward Dunsinane. Arm, arm, and out!
If this which he avouches does appear,   *if its true, I cant*
There is nor flying hence nor tarrying here. *stay, but I cant*
I 'gin to be aweary of the sun   *leave*
55   And wish the estate[72] o' the world were now undone.
Ring the alarum bell! Blow, wind! Come, wrack![73]
At least we'll die with harness[74] on our back.

regrets killing duncan
tired of everything
okay with dying.

                Exeunt.

[71]decrease

[72]present state

[73]ruin

[74]armor

SCENE VI
[Dunsinane. Before the castle.]

attacking castle

Drum and colors. *Enter Malcolm, Siward, Macduff, and their*
Army, with boughs.

MALCOLM: Now near enough; your leafy screens throw down,   *throw*
And show like those you are. You, worthy uncle,   *down the leaves*
Shall, with my cousin, your right noble son,   *close enough*
Lead our first battle.[75] Worthy Macduff and we   *now*
Shall take upon's what else remains to do,
According to our order.
5   SIWARD: Fare you well.
Do we but find the tyrant's power tonight,
Let us be beaten, if we cannot fight.
MACDUFF: Make all our trumpets speak; give them all breath,
Those clamorous harbingers of blood and death.

they all bringers of blood + death

         Exeunt. Alarums continued.

[75]battalion

SCENE VII
[Another part of the field.]

Enter Macbeth.

MACBETH: They have tied me to a stake; I cannot fly,
   But bear-like[76] I must fight the course. What's he
   That was not born of woman? Such a one
   Am I to fear, or none.

Enter young Siward.

5 YOUNG SIWARD: What is thy name?
   MACBETH: Thou'lt be afraid to hear it.
   YOUNG SIWARD: No, though thou call'st thyself a hotter name
   Than any is in hell.
   MACBETH: My name's Macbeth.
10 YOUNG SIWARD: The devil himself could not pronounce a title
   More hateful to mine ear.
   MACBETH: No, nor more fearful.
   YOUNG SIWARD: Thou liest, abhorred tyrant; with my sword
   I'll prove the lie thou speak'st.

[They] fight, and young Siward slain.

15 MACBETH: Thou wast born of woman.
   But swords I smile at, weapons laugh to scorn,
   Brandish'd by man that's of a woman born.   *Exit.*

Alarums. Enter Macduff.

MACDUFF: That way the noise is. Tyrant, show thy face!
   If thou beest slain and with no stroke of mine,
20 My wife and children's ghosts will haunt me still.[77]
   I cannot strike at wretched kerns, whose arms
   Are hired to bear their staves.[78] Either thou, Macbeth,
   Or else my sword, with an unbatter'd edge,
   I sheathe again undeeded.[79] There thou shouldst be;
25 By this great clatter, one of greatest note
   Seems bruited.[80] Let me find him, fortune!
   And more I beg not.   *Exit. Alarums.*

[76] [In bearbaiting, a common Elizabethan entertainment, dogs were loosed upon a bear tied to a stake.]

[77] always

[78] sticks, clubs

[79] unused

[80] announced

[Handwritten annotations:]
Kills Siward
eventhough Siward wanted to kill him
becomes confident in prophecy still
Avenge his family

Enter Malcolm and Siward.

SIWARD: This way, my lord; the castle's gently render'd.[81]

30   The tyrant's people on both sides do fight,
The noble thanes do bravely in the war;
The day almost itself professes yours,
And little is to do.
MALCOLM: We have met with foes
35   That strike beside us.[82]
SIWARD: Enter, sir, the castle.

Exeunt. Alarum.

[81]surrendered

[82]fight beside us

(handwritten: castle surrendered)

[SCENE VIII]
[Another part of the field.]

Enter Macbeth.

MACBETH: Why should I play the Roman fool[83] and die
On mine own sword? Whiles I see lives,[84] the gashes[85]
Do better upon them.

Enter Macduff.

MACDUFF: Turn, hell hound, turn!
5   MACBETH: Of all men else I have avoided thee.
But get thee back; my soul is too much charged
With blood of thine already.
MACDUFF: I have no words:
My voice is in my sword, thou bloodier villain
10   Than terms[86] can give thee out! [87]   *Fight: Alarum.*
MACBETH: Thou losest labor.[88]
As easy mayst thou the intrenchant[89] air
With thy keen sword impress[90] as make me bleed:
Let fall thy blade on vulnerable crests;
15   I bear a charmed life, which must not yield
To one of woman born.
MACDUFF: Despair thy charm,

[83]a soldier who
commits suicide
rather than be
captured or other-
wise dishonored

[84]people living

[85]sword cuts

[86]words

[87]describe you

[88]waste your effort

[89]unable to be cut

[90]mark

(handwritten: he already killed your whole fam. I don't want to kill you too)

(handwritten: your blade may fall on me but I am charmed)

[handwritten: Macduff was born early Mother died in birth.]

[91] evil spirit

And let the angel[91] whom thou still hast served

Tell thee, Macduff was from his mother's womb

[92] prematurely

20   Untimely[92] ripp'd.[93] [handwritten: last prophecy.]

[handwritten: wasn't teen. born from woman]

[93] removed by Caesarian section

[handwritten: realized double meaning]

MACBETH: Accursed be that tongue that tells me so,

[94] tamed

For it hath cow'd[94] my better part of man!

And be these juggling fiends no more believed,

[95] act misleadingly or insincerely

That palter[95] with us in a double sense,

25   That keep the word of promise to our ear,

And break it to our hope. I'll not fight with thee.

MACDUFF: Then yield thee, coward,

And live to be the show and gaze[96] o' the time.

[96] spectacle

We'll have thee, as our rarer monsters are,

[97] painted on posters

30   Painted upon a pole,[97] and underwrit,

[handwritten: cut off his head and put it on a po]

"Here may you see the tyrant."

MACBETH: I will not yield,

To kiss the ground before young Malcolm's feet,

And to be baited[98] with the rabble's curse.

[98] tormented with insults

[handwritten: I will not bow to Malcom]

35   Though Birnam Wood be come to Dunsinane,

And thou opposed, being of no woman born,

Yet I will try the last. Before my body

I throw my warlike shield! Lay on, Macduff,

And damn'd be him that first cries, "Hold, enough!"

          Exeunt fighting. Alarums.

[handwritten: Macduff killed Macbeth as promise]

Enter fighting, and Macbeth slain. Retreat.[99] Flourish. Enter,

[99] This indicates a specific trumpet call, not a physical movement.

with drum and colors, Malcolm, Siward, Ross, [the other]

Thanes, and Soldiers.

40   MALCOLM: I would[100] the friends we miss were safe arrived.

SIWARD: Some must go off:[101] and yet, by these[102] I see,

[100] wish

So great a day as this is cheaply bought.

MALCOLM: Macduff is missing, and your noble son.

[101] perish

ROSS: Your son, my lord, has paid a soldier's debt:

[102] the many soldiers here

45   He only lived but till he was a man;

The which no sooner had his prowess confirm'd

[103] unyielding position

In the unshrinking station[103] where he fought,

But like a man he died. [handwritten: young Siward]

SIWARD: Then he is dead?

50   ROSS: Ay, and brought off the field. Your cause of sorrow

Must not be measured by his worth, for then

It hath no end.

SIWARD: Had he his hurts before?[104]

ROSS: Ay, on the front.

SIWARD: Why then, God's soldier be he!

55   Had I as many sons as I have hairs,

I would not wish them to a fairer death.

And so his knell is knoll'd.

MALCOLM: He's worth more sorrow,

And that I'll spend for him.

60 SIWARD: He's worth no more:

They say he parted well and paid his score:

And so God be with him! Here comes newer comfort.

[Re]-enter Macduff, with Macbeth's head.

MACDUFF: Hail, King! for so thou art. Behold where stands

The usurper's cursed head. The time is free.

65   I see thee compass'd with thy kingdom's pearl[105]

That speak my salutation in their minds,

Whose voices I desire aloud with mine:

Hail, King of Scotland!

ALL: Hail, King of Scotland!   *Flourish.*

70 MALCOLM: We shall not spend a large expense of time

Before we reckon[106] with your several loves,[107]

And make us even with[108] you. My thanes and kinsmen,

Henceforth be Earls, the first that ever Scotland

In such an honor named. What's more to do,

75   Which would[109] be planted newly with the time,[110]

As calling home our exiled friends abroad

That fled the snares of watchful tyranny,

Producing forth[111] the cruel ministers

Of this dead butcher and his fiend-like queen,

80   Who, as 'tis thought, by self[112] and violent hands

Took off her life; this, and what needful else

That calls upon us, by the grace of Grace

We will perform in measure,[113] time, and place,

So thanks to all at once and to each one,

85   Whom we invite to see us crown'd at Scone.

Flourish. Exeunt.

[104] *on his front side*

[105] *noblemen*

[106] *consider*

[107] *loyal efforts*

[108] *i.e., reward your service*

[109] *should*

[110] *new era*

[111] *Bringing to trial*

[112] *her own*

[113] *in due order*

VOCABULARY AND GLOSSARY

Dramatis Personae
thane – a feudal Scottish title equivalent to baron
Northumberland – the northernmost county in England
Apparitions – ghostly figures

Act I, Scene I
—

Act I, Scene II
plight – an unfortunate or difficult situation
villainies – treacherous acts; the Sergeant uses this term in reference to the mercenaries hired by the Norwegian king to invade Scotland.
Hebrides – a group of islands of northwestern Scotland; Norwegians conquered the islands and ruled until 1266, and Scottish chieftains ruled until the sixteenth century.
kerns – lightly armed, medieval Scottish or Irish footsoldiers
gallowglasses – heavily armed Irish horsemen
disdaining – regarding with contempt; feeling scornful
minion – a servile follower
battlements – a parapet on top of a castle wall with notches through which weapons can be fired in defense
direful – causing fear or dread; the time after the spring equinox is also the season of storms.
Golgotha – a hill near Jerusalem where Jesus was crucified, also known as Calvary; it is usually translated as "place of skulls."
dismal – causing depression; dreary
proof – armor heavy enough to deflect arrows
deign – to do something that one considers to be below oneself; to condescend to
disburse – to pay out; to expend
Saint Colme's Inch – Inchcolm, an island in the Firth of Forth in Scotland
firth – a long, narrow inlet of the sea

Act I, Scene III
compass card – a navigation device used by early mariners. It consists of
  magnetic needles mounted to a freely rotating circular disk.
hereafter – in the immediate future
enkindle – to rouse into action
earnest – showing deep sincerity or seriousness
wrought – worked up

Act I, Scene IV
commission – an authorization to perform certain tasks or duties
recompense – repayment; compensation
enfold – to wrap up; to enclose
peerless – having no match; incomparable

Act I, Scene V
ambition – a strong desire to achieve
chastise – 1. to punish by inflicting pain 2. to criticize severely
impedes – hinders; obstructs progress
tidings – news or information
compunctious – having pangs of doubt or guilt (compunctions)
gall – bile, the bitter digestive juice secreted by the gall bladder
sway – power; influence; authority
masterdom – rule; authority over others

Act I, Scene VI
jutty – a decorative or architectural projection of a building that overhangs
  the wall below
purveyor – one who procures and supplies provisions, especially food

Act I, Scene VII
chalice – a bowl-shaped drinking cup; a goblet
virtues – moral excellence; admirable qualities
cherubin (Cherubim) – a winged angel; in Christianity, the second-highest
  rank of angels
prithee – please ("pray thee")
chamberlains – servants in charge of a particular part of an estate

Act II, Scene I

repose – rest, relaxation

augment – to increase something in size, amount, or degree; to make greater

palpable – capable of being touched or felt; tangible

Hecate – the goddess of witchcraft of Greek myth; originally the goddess of fertility, Hecate later became the queen of Hades and the protector of witches.

sentinel – a guard; a sentry

Tarquin – the prince of Roman myth who raped Lucrece, a woman famous for her matronly virtue

prate – to talk idly; to babble without purpose

knell – the sound of a bell toll, especially one signaling a funeral

Act II, Scene II

—

Act II, Scene III

Belzebub (Beelzebub) – the name given to the Devil

primrose – 1. a wildflower of varying color 2. flowery; pleasant

lechery – excessive indulgence in lust or self pleasure

equivocator – one who intentionally speaks vaguely; the Jesuit order believed that a false statement was not a lie if it was meant to have a particular meaning. Father Garnett, a Jesuit, unsuccessfully used this belief as a defense during his trial for treason in 1606.

equivocate – to be intentionally ambiguous or unclear in order to mislead or withhold information

requited – to repaid either benignly, as one would for a good deed, or punitively, as for revenge

lamentings – expressions of grief; mourning

sacrilegious – irreverent toward something held to be sacred

Gorgon – in Greek myth, a monster having a woman's body and snakes for hair whose glance turned people into stone; Medusa was a Gorgon.

steep'd – [steeped] soaked in liquid; saturated

malice – the desire to cause harm to others; hatefulness

consort – to be in agreement; to associate with

Act II, Scene IV

score – a group of twenty

Act III, Scene I
verity – truth
oracle – a person or entity that predicts the future
indissoluble – not capable of being dissolved; permanent
parricide – the murder of one's own mother, father, or near relative
dauntless – incapable of being discouraged; intrepid
Mark Antony – Mark Antony and Octavius Caesar were members of the
    Second Triumvirate, a group of three rulers of Rome; Shakespeare's plays
    Antony and Cleopatra and *Julius Caesar* feature them as characters.
chid – scolded
scepter – a staff or mace carried by a king or queen
wrought – worked
subtle – difficult to detect or perceive
incensed – enraged; extremely angry
botches – mistakes made due to clumsiness

Act III, Scene II
assailable – capable of being attacked; undefended
cloister'd – [cloistered] A *cloister* is a place devoted to religious seclusion,
    such as a monastery or convent. Here the word means *secret*.

Act III, Scene III

——

Act III, Scene IV
mirth – festivity; merriment
charnel houses – tombs or vaults for the bones of the dead; originally,
    these held remains that were uncovered or displaced when new graves
    were dug.
augures [*auguries*] – omens; predictions of the future; an *augur* is a seer or
    prophet.

Act III, Scene V
wayward – resistant to guidance; unpredictable; directionless
wrought – conducted

Act III, Scene VI

malevolence – wishing evil or injury to others

exasperate – to make angry; to annoy

rue – to feel sorrow; to regret

Act IV, Scene I

gibbet – a gallows or similar structure for public execution

deftly – with skill and dexterity

potent – having inner power or force

chafes – annoys; angers

vanquish'd – [*vanquished*] defeated or conquered in battle or conflict

pernicious – highly destructive, injurious, or fatal

aye – always

Act IV, Scene II

diminutive – very small in size or value; insignificant

laudable – worthy of praise; commendable

Act IV, Scene III

grafted – closely united

avaricious – extremely greedy

malicious – having hatred or ill will

voluptuousness – state of being devoted to sensual pleasures

matrons – wives, widows, or motherly women

maids – change to unmarried girls or women

cistern – a tank or reservoir for holding water or other liquids

impediments – obstructions; things that hinder progress

intemperance – excess in drinking alcohol or eating

perseverance – persisting in an undertaking despite any opposition

blaspheme – to use the name of God in an disrespectful manner

integrity – strict adherence to a moral code

credulous – believing too easily; gullible

detraction – a derogatory comment about a person's reputation

abjure – to formally renounce or recant

coveted – greatly desired

sanctity – sacredness; holiness

benediction – a blessing

Act V, Scene I

—

Act V, Scene II
upbraid – to reproach; to reprimand

Act V, Scene III
raze – to erase; to obliterate

Act V, Scene IV
industrious – diligent in work or study; assiduous

Act V, Scene V
—

Act V, Scene VI
—

Act V, Scene VII
—

Act V, Scene VIII
—

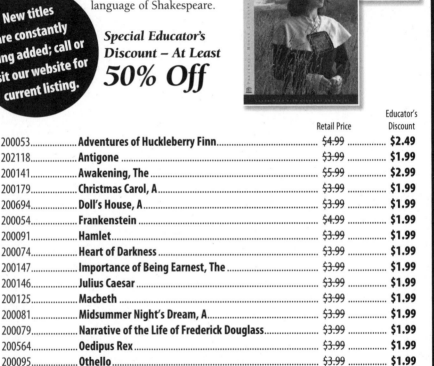